SHAKESPEAR
TRUTH AND TRADITION

BY

JOHN SEMPLE SMART, M.A., D.Litt.

(LATE LECTURER ON ENGLISH LITERATURE IN THE
UNIVERSITY OF GLASGOW)

WITH A MEMOIR BY

W. MACNEILE DIXON

REGIUS PROFESSOR OF ENGLISH LITERATURE IN THE
UNIVERSITY OF GLASGOW

'"Onorate l'altissimo poeta:
l'ombra sua torna, ch'era dipartita'"

LONDON
EDWARD ARNOLD & CO.

First published, 1928
Reprinted 1929

Made and Printed in Great Britain by
Butler & Tanner Ltd., Frome and London

Kessinger Publishing's Rare Reprints
Thousands of Scarce and Hard-to-Find Books!

THE GRAFTON PORTRAIT OF SHAKESPEARE
IN THE JOHN RYLANDS LIBRARY, MANCHESTER

CONTENTS

PORTRAITS

JOHN SEMPLE SMART

A MEMOIR OF THE AUTHOR

Among the scholars of his own generation John Semple Smart attracted little attention. His lot should have fallen in an age earlier than his own ; he should have walked the cloisters of an ancient college. There was a kind of piety in his learning, a flavour of the past, a pleasant absence of modernity. He had an artist's distaste for things half done, or of no quality, and was modestly content, while others with far less knowledge bestrode the public stage, to add patiently to his own stock. He never hastened with his wares to market, or announced their value. Old fashioned, a trifle, in manner, courteous and unobtrusive, in every way lettered and a gentleman, his leisurely and precise methods became him. They were in keeping with the natural aristocracy of his tastes. He took no pleasure in hurried generalizations, preferred the best and had no sort of belief " that excellence was common and abundant." The last duty of a scholar was, he conceived, display, the first, exactness, and he would for patient years await a fact to complete the argument, or to justify a conclusion already, he believed, secure.

Almost a solitary, who thought and worked in sturdy

independence, in the atmosphere of books, a bachelor's isolation, he was not less happy among chosen friends and delighted in discussion. But in the study, passing mere opinions by, he reserved all his respect for originals, and spent in consequence many dusty hours in search of documents, or among forgotten books, with Parish registers or Municipal records. Of his admirable type few are left us, and fewer still will follow, for he was wisely learned rather than a specialist, a shining example of true as opposed to false learning, a lover of beauty, a man with all Western culture as his province, to whom famous pictures were as familiar as famous books, at ease when there was talk of the masterpieces in poetry, art or philosophy, of Delphi or Florence, of Palladio, Dante or the Dialogues of Hume.

Smart's literary ancestry went back, we are told, to his maternal grandfather, whose name he bore. A portrait of John Semple shows a face of singular beauty and refinement, framed in white hair, a face with just such a touch of mysticism and other-world-liness as might be seen in his grandson's. To that ancestor, a zealous Covenanter, who was accustomed every Sabbath to walk four miles to his little Cameronian church, and whose books were the Bible, Bunyan and Baxter, might be traced, too, something of his physique and character, of his purity and austerity of mind.

In opinions a child of the Renaissance, and a devout believer in the civilization which has its roots in the arts and literature of Greece and Rome, Smart, like his favourite Milton, was not less a staunch friend of the Reformation, and I can recall the smile with which he would quote from the *Amours de Voyage* :—

" Luther, they say, was unwise ; he didn't see how things
    were going ;
Luther was foolish,—but, O great God ! what call you
    Ignatius ? "

The picture of patient misery in foolish company, when he had an attentive listener he was full of matter, and never dull though often silent. It was necessary, indeed, to angle for his judgments, but a dexterous cast rarely failed to secure a penetrating comment, a sentence of price.

For some of us there lay a peculiar charm in the quietness of his manner, though many were betrayed by the simplicity of his style into supposing that to be an index to simplicity of mind which was but a veil over profound reflection, and the widest acquaintance with all the details of his subject. A sensitive delicacy, a propriety of judgment in matters literary, joined with an unfailing lucidity and a tincture of irony, gave an Addisonian quality to his discourses, as in his quiet commentary on Hardy's sentence, so quiet as to be easily overlooked :—

" ' Justice was done, and the President of the Immortals, in Æschylean phrase, had finished his sport with Tess.'

" The phrase ' President of the Immortals,' " he remarks, " has indeed been translated from Æschylus ; but

' ended his sport ' is Hardy's own." How smooth, how swift and sure a thrust !

Born at Port Glasgow in 1868, Smart, on the death of his parents, resided with relatives at St. Andrews, where, at Madras College, he won a bursary, which took him to the University. With the aid of tutorial and other work he completed his course in 1894, graduating with the Tyndale Bruce Scholarship and First Class Honours in Philosophy. A year or so later an essay which won the Lord Rector's Gold Medal, presented by Lord Dufferin, brought him to the notice of Mr. R. C. Munro-Ferguson (then M.P. for Leith and afterwards Lord Novar) and for three years Smart served as his private secretary. His philosophical studies at the University were followed by literary and linguistic studies in France, Germany and Italy. A summer session at the Sorbonne and later visits to Paris laid the foundations of his intimate knowledge of French History and literature, and the winter of 1898 at the University of Jena, when he attended the lectures of philosophers and philologers, among others those of Dr. Wolfgang Kellar, gave him his familiarity with German. But his heart was with Italy, a country for which he had an almost passionate attachment, and to which he returned again and again with undiminished enthusiasm. Other vacations were spent in Greece or among the Alps, and he was never more delightfully himself than in conversation which recalled the scenes and incidents of travel in classic lands.

During one winter Smart lectured at McGill University, Montreal, and later taught at Ayr and Glasgow academies.

In 1907 he was appointed to the English staff at the University of Glasgow, as Queen Margaret College Lecturer, a post which he held until his death in 1925. In 1912 he received the degree of Doctor of Letters from his own University of St. Andrews.

Though his writings may be adjudged deficient in quantity, in quality they are beyond reproach. His book on *James Macpherson*, a survey of the Ossian controversy, and his edition of *The Sonnets of Milton* remain without rivals. If, a sufferer from the scholar's malady, fastidiousness, he has left comparatively little, that little may be accepted with gratitude and without suspicion. He aimed at truth, and his name is worthy to be entered in the right honourable society of the trustworthy. Smart's work upon Shakespeare was cut short by his death, and the present book lacks, in consequence, three vital chapters—those in which he proposed to deal with the more difficult and still unsettled textual problems. But it presents the dramatist as he saw him in the setting of the times, a natural and convincing portrait of a man in whom his acquaintances and contemporaries saw nothing to excite special enquiry; nothing astonishing in their good friend save his genius, nothing abnormal in his career save its most excellent achievements.

To Smart's friend and successor in the Queen Margaret College Lectureship, Mr. Peter Alexander, we owe the transcription of the pencilled chapters and notes, a labour of love, which made it possible to send this book to the press. Written often on stray sheets, within and without the ordinary limits of the page, they were sometimes difficult to decipher, and had, of course, never received the author's final revision.

The portrait is from a pencil drawing of 1896, the work of Mr. William Urwick.

W. MACNEILE DIXON.

NOTE ON THE FRONTISPIECE

The portrait of a young man, styled the *Grafton Portrait of Shakespeare*, was discovered in 1907 at Darlington. It was purchased by the late Mr. Thomas Kay, and presented by him to the John Rylands Library, Manchester, where it now hangs. Painted on an oak panel, it bears the inscription

Æ SVÆ 24, 1588,

and is allowed to be a work of that date. The inscribed age corresponds with that of Shakespeare in the year mentioned, and the painting as a whole resembles the Droeshout in certain interesting features. It cannot be claimed with any certainty as an authentic portrait of the dramatist, but was greatly admired by the author of the present volume, who found in it his own idea of the youthful Shakespeare, and wished it genuine. A full account of its history may be read in *The Story of the Grafton Portrait of William Shakespeare*, by Thomas Kay (Partridge & Co., London, 1914).

I

INTRODUCTION

Shakespeare's biography was not written in his own time, nor in the generation that followed it, by anyone who had known him personally or even by anyone receiving information from his friends. For this omission nothing is to be blamed but the general incuriosity of the age. Biography as practised to-day had not yet been invented. It has since become both a branch of literature and an exact and accurate study; no labour is now deemed too great to recover any significant fact in the lives of famous men of the past. But such interest and inquiry are of modern origin. In the seventeenth century the works of a great poet might be loved and his name revered; but his admirers cared little to know the occupation of his father, or the school where he studied in his youth, or the names of his wife and children, or his disposition and temperament, or his private hopes, fears and ambitions, or his happy sallies in intimate talk. It was Boswell who first conceived the idea of a comprehensive biography in which the whole personality of his hero should be revealed. There was no Boswell for Shakespeare.

In this respect he shared the common lot, and was not more neglected than other great poets. The life of Edmund Spenser is more obscure than his. Nothing is known of Spenser's youth except that he was a native of London and was educated at Merchant Taylors' School. We do not know the date of his birth or the Christian name of his father, or the street or parish where he resided ; although in the case of Shakespeare the corresponding facts are familiar. Spenser entered the service of the Government and from official reports a few details about him can be gleaned ; but towards the close darkness settles down again, and the circumstances of his death are still involved in mystery. Milton has been almost as unfortunate as Shakespeare. What is most certainly known of his life and character is derived from the autobiographical passages in his own prose works. The first published biography was written by his nephew, Edward Phillips, long after his death, and apparently in the most casual manner. The narrative is very brief—it extends only to a few printed pages,—and it has been done with such indifference to accuracy that Phillips is wrong even in the dates of his uncle's birth and death. Interesting anecdotes or characteristic sayings of Milton may be sought for there in vain.

With Dryden the story repeats itself. When Dr. Johnson undertook to write the life of Dryden, he began it with these words :—

" Of the great poet whose life I am about to delineate, the curiosity which his reputation must excite, will require a display more ample than can now be given. His contemporaries, however they reverenced his genius, left his life unwritten ; and nothing, therefore, can be known beyond what casual mention and uncertain tradition have supplied."

These are words which might be placed at the beginning of every life of Shakespeare.

The indifference to biographical interest which prevailed in Shakespeare's time was of long continuation ; and was dispelled only towards the close of the eighteenth century and the beginning of the nineteenth. There are no comprehensive biographies of any English authors before Boswell's *Life of Johnson*, Lockhart's *Life of Scott*, and Moore's *Life of Byron*. Even the friends of Addison and Pope forgot to put their history on record before it was too late ; and the lives of both these authors are now very imperfectly known.

The first life of Shakespeare which found its way into print was written, nearly a hundred years after his death, by Nicholas Rowe. Its author, who was a popular dramatist in the time of Queen Anne, published an edition of Shakespeare's works, and prefixed to the first volume a brief account of his career. Rowe had taken very little trouble. He had not even gone to Stratford-on-Avon to see the poet's birthplace for himself, and was contented with such information as his friend, Betterton, had picked up there during a brief visit, and with such tales as were circulating in his own time in London. Rowe made no attempt to obtain access to State papers, which might throw light on Shakespeare's connection with the Court, and knew nothing of the royal patent appointing him and his fellow-actors as Players to the

King, which was printed a few years afterwards in Rymer's *Fœdera*. And he makes no mention of Shakespeare's will, or of the documents at Heralds' College concerning his coat-of-arms.

Slight and inaccurate as it was, Rowe's story was deemed sufficient for all purposes; and was quietly reproduced in one edition of Shakespeare after another for a hundred years. Some account of the dramatist must be prefixed to the volumes. What could be better, thought the editors, than Mr. Rowe's excellent narrative, and what more easy to reprint?

Modern Shakespearian scholarship made its effective beginning with Edmund Malone. That illustrious man, whose services to the poet's memory cannot be sufficiently valued, was a friend of Johnson and Boswell. It was his ambition to do for Shakespeare what Boswell did for Johnson; but by the only means then available, antiquarian research. Every fragment of information that could be discovered by the most painstaking inquiry was collected; traditions and dubious tales were tested by critical methods and the outline of a sound and accurate biography of Shakespeare was laid down. But Malone's work has one serious defect. It was not written with the literary art and imaginative insight which attract the public; it made no popular appeal, and was read only by scholars. Despite the research and sound judgment that had gone to its making, it had little influence upon the general notions of Shakespeare's life.

A Shakespeare legend had been gradually and almost

unconsciously created, and had taken firm possession of the public mind. It is easily indicated by the words which David Hume used in his History of England to describe the poet. Shakespeare was " born in a rude age and educated in the lowest manner, without any instruction from the world or from books." And in detail the legend presented Shakespeare in an even less flattering light. He was a man gravely hampered by his origin and early surroundings. His father was a simple tradesman, usually called a butcher, who met with financial disaster, and could do nothing to help his son. Shakespeare was taken early from school, after a most limited and imperfect education, and apprenticed to his father's business. He fell into trouble with a neighbouring landlord, Sir Thomas Lucy, who prosecuted him for poaching, and was forced to flee from his home to London ; arrived there in a friendless and forlorn condition, and made a living at first by holding horses in the streets ; then became a servant or call-boy at a theatre, and was admitted among the actors. His superiors in the company discovered that he had literary gifts, and employed him to tinker and repatch old plays. He gradually made fame and fortune as a dramatist, acquired property, returned to Stratford and died there. He was so careless of his works that they would have been left to perish, had they not been rescued from destruction by two of his fellow-actors, who gave them to the press. As for learning and cultivation, he had practically none, and knew no language but his own, unless a slight smattering of Latin grammar might be conceded.

B

Early in the nineteenth century began the Romantic Movement, which had an almost universal influence on poetry and criticism. This is not the place to discuss the Romantic Movement; we are concerned with it only as it may have affected the common estimate of Shakespeare's life and character. The Romantic writers looked upon all great men with profound reverence and wonder, and sought to make a miracle of their very existence. They even idealized the poet until no place could be found for him in the everyday world of common folk, where he must after all have lived, for the poet is not a man in a book. Shakespeare was subjected to this idealizing process, and was placed on a pinnacle far above all other writers, however illustrious. Emerson has declared that Shakespeare is not to be judged " by the common measure of great authors, such as Bacon, Milton, Tasso and Cervantes." As he was greater than all these, we must look for some higher significance in his life than in theirs.

We can but ask in some astonishment why such an assumption should be made. Why should great men of letters be divided into two classes,—Shakespeare by himself in the first, and all others in the second; and why should we set up for Shakespeare a standard of elevation in private life which we do not ask of the rest ? Why should Shakespeare be so unlike Milton that we look in his biography for marvels and mysteries unspeakable, whilst we are content to allow that Milton may have lived amongst ordinary affairs like an ordinary man. The creation of an ethereal Shakespeare, incomprehensively grand and remote, had dangers which were not suspected. When he had become too ethereal for real life, only one step remained to be taken—to make him fade away altogether.

But the Romantics did something even more perilous. With their veneration for Shakespeare it might have been expected that they would cast aside the story of the butcher's apprentice and the runaway poacher; and would reject even more decisively the young author whose services were first used by his employers in the cobbling of other men's work. But it was not so. The legendary tales continued in being and were invested with new significance. They seemed to throw Shakespeare's greatness into higher relief.

Those who make a close study of the Romantic Movement may detect in it a vein of paradox, a love of picturesque and startling antithesis. Sometimes the Romanticists dwell on the contrast between exquisite artistic feeling and moral callousness, united in a single person, as Browning has done in more poems than one. Sometimes they present a character who is in truth a modest and self-sacrificing hero, but who is placed in circumstances so strange that public opinion condemns him for a scoundrel. This is the case of Browning's Caponsacchi, and of Victor Hugo's Jean Valjean, who is to the uninitiated a desperate ruffian, a mere escaped convict, and to the initiated a noble human spirit. Or the paradox might take another but not altogether dissimilar form. It might be made by contrasting a poet's achievements with his circumstances, the apparently incon-

gruous being overcome in a higher glory. Burns was
both an illiterate ploughman and his country's greatest
son. He was, says Carlyle, " one of those men who
reach down to the perennial deeps, who take rank with
the Heroic among men ; and he was born in a poor
Ayrshire hut. The largest soul of all the British lands
came among us in the shape of a hard-handed Scottish
Peasant."

It seemed an easy transition from Burns to Shakespeare.
In him also poor beginnings and a rude adventurous
youth were supposed to augment the miracle of poetic
power. The contrast glorified his amplitude of intellect
and imagination, his incomparable original genius.
Knowing the reversion which was soon to follow we
now read with sadness the raptures of Carlyle over " our
poor Warwickshire Peasant, who rose to be manager of
a Playhouse, so that he could live without begging, . . .
whom Sir Thomas Lucy was for sending to the tread-
mill,"—who would never have thought of poetry, if
Lucy had let him alone,—but who is none the less the
greatest thing we have yet done, whom we would not
give in exchange for an Indian Empire, the Hero-Poet
the articulate voice of England.

Then, in natural sequence, arose another school of
critics, who began where the Romantics had left off,
and took over their results. They accepted Shakespeare
the inaccessible and superhuman genius ; and they
accepted Shakespeare the man from Stratford of humble
origin and dubious antecedents. They held fast on one
hand to the ethereal poet, and on the other to the young

barbarian ; but they disputed their identity. With more shrewdness than the romantic Shakespearians had displayed, they perceived an irreconcilable incongruity between them ; but they saw no means of grappling with the enigma except by disjoining them altogether. It was impossible that the poet and the man from Stratford could be the same. That the stories told of Shakespeare were unfounded, that he had never actually passed through the unhappy experiences attributed to him, that his youth and early manhood contained nothing inconsistent with the manifestation of literary power, was the true solution of the puzzle, and offered the only safe and certain way out. A drastic revision of the traditional biography would have removed all difficulties. But the new critics did not enter on the plain path to reality. They also were under the spell of romanticism and paradox. A more daring romanticism and an even more incredible paradox occurred with blinding fascination to their minds. They separated Shakespeare from his works altogether and looked round for another to whom they might be attributed. Francis Bacon, whose laborious philosophical works very few of his new admirers had ever read, presented himself to their fancy ; he was hailed as a universal genius capable of all things ; and the laurels were placed upon his brow.

Since the first steps were taken there has been an astonishing development. Baconism has grown into a creed ; it has its fervent devotees and its impassioned rhetoric ; its denunciations of our greatest poet are now familiar to an ever wider circle of readers. With cheery contemptuousness it sees in all the admirers of Shakespeare, from his Elizabethan and Jacobean friends, who knew him personally, to the present day, only a set of muddle-headed cranks called Stratfordians. The case against the poet has been much elaborated. It begins with lively aspersions on his life and conduct in which the stories told of his humble origin are dwelt on with a strange harshness of tone, exploited and magnified in a manner only too reminiscent of that old-fashioned social intolerance which is now called snobbery. His family and friends all suffer alike. Shakespeare, it is said, spent his early years like honest Ovid among the Goths. His parents and townspeople were vulgar and illiterate. He is the Stratford rustic; the young provincial; the peasant; the boor; the clown. How is it possible, ask the Baconians, with triumphant incredulity, that a young man brought up in a remote country district, amongst ignorant louts, possessing only the wretched manners to be acquired there, with a deplorable accent, without the slightest tinge of scholarship or acquaintance with good breeding, could become the author of works so noble and refined, so full of erudition, and showing such familiarity with the ways of cultivated society.

Shakespeare being thus got rid of, Bacon is put in his place: it is not easy to understand why. England had a large population and two Universities; its intellectual life was brilliant and inspired with a new vigour; there were multitudes of men who possessed both industry and mental power. Why if Shakespeare is debarred, and quietly removed from the scene, should Bacon, more

than any other, step into the vacant place ? No satis-
factory reply has ever been given to this question. It
is assumed that the choice of candidates lies obviously
between Shakespeare and Bacon ; and that, Shakespeare
being eliminated, Bacon alone remains. When a reason
is offered it possesses no serious weight. A familiar line of
argument exists which may be briefly expressed in this
fashion : the tragedies and comedies attributed to
Shakespeare abound in classical allusions, are steeped in
classical learning, can have been written only by a great
classical scholar ; Bacon was the greatest classical scholar
of the age ; therefore Bacon was the author.

This inference rests on two premises, both of which
may be disputed. The classical learning shown in the
plays is not profound ; there is a rare cultivation of
mind, an exquisite refinement of literary taste ; but
extensive and accurate reading in the Greek and Latin
literatures, amounting to erudition, is not traceable ; there
is nothing even to establish with certainty that the author
of the plays possessed any knowledge of Greek at all.
And Bacon's own reputation as a classical scholar is the
creation of his modern and misguided admirers. He
wrote with ease and fluency in Latin, and had a solid
mastery of the language ; but so had hundreds of other
Englishmen. His acquaintance with Greek cannot have
been easy and familiar ; for he habitually read Greek
authors in Latin translations. In *The Advancement of
Learning* he quotes Homer, Pindar, and Demosthenes in
Latin, with nothing to indicate that Latin was not their
mother tongue.

By rejecting Shakespeare's authorship the Baconians believe themselves to be eliminating something wildly improbable,—the ignorant and untutored rustic developing into a great poet. But they have put in its place something more improbable still. Anyone who reads Bacon's *Essays* and *The Advancement of Learning*, and then *Midsummer Night's Dream* and *The Merchant of Venice*, will hardly conclude that all these works must have been written by the same person. He will find it easy to believe that the *Essays* and *The Advancement of Learning* came from one and the same hand. He will observe a likeness, indeed an identity in the prose style, a similar attitude of mind and similar trains of thought ; he will find himself in presence of the same intellect. Turning to *Midsummer Night's Dream* and *The Merchant of Venice*, he will find in both the same form and movement in the verse, the same imaginative glow, the same playful wit, the same sweetness, harmony and grace. He will naturally believe that the two prose works were written by one man, and that the two poems were written by one man ; but between the prose works and the poems he will find a wholly irreconcilable difference. They have nothing in common except the use of the English language.

Thus the Baconians get rid of one miracle only to substitute another. They set up a writer of such universal and all comprehensive genius, such amazing versatility, that he has no parallel in the history of literature.

Perceiving the weakness of the ground, some writers, after rejecting Shakespeare's claims, refuse to commit themselves to Bacon's. They contend more cautiously for a Great Unknown. There were two William Shakespeares, both in London at the same time and about the same age. The first was born at Stratford, became an actor, made money, and retired to his native town. The second wrote the plays; and all that can be said of him is that he wrote the plays. Even his real name may be one of the secrets of history; for William Shakespeare may have been only a pseudonym which completely deceived the world, leaving his identity to be for ever beyond our ken.

The train of reasoning pursued by the sceptics leads to singular results. The life of a great poet, they argue, must needs excite the interest of his contemporaries, and become familiar to posterity through the narratives which they put on record; and therefore it is impossible to admit that any man could be a great poet, if we are ignorant of his personal history. It is true that nothing, not even his birthplace or the century in which he was born, can be established about Homer; but Homer lived some thousands of years ago, and Shakespeare only three hundred. Concerning him we might expect a wealth of information. Had the man of Stratford been a genuine poet, his biography could not have been left imperfect. Our curiosity about him would have been amply satisfied. But his actual life is wrapped in oblivion. Questions are asked to which no scholar can reply. Shakespeare is the man of mystery, the elusive phantom, and as a great author is impossible and incredible.

To fill the vacancy the sceptics suggest another individual who is even more mysterious, elusive and phantasmal. The real origin of the plays is given up as a hopeless problem. Nothing can be told of the author of *Hamlet* and *Othello* except that he lived and wrote in the time of Elizabeth and James I, and left no other trace of his presence upon earth. Having disposed of Shakespeare because we know so little about him, the sceptics put in his place an authentic and marvellous writer, about whom we know absolutely nothing at all. They forget the assumption with which they began, and end the argument in complete self-contradiction.

Familiar conceptions of Shakespeare are deeply involved in such paradoxes. He is the great poet who was also a great ignoramus ; the great visionary who cared only for cash ; the great man of letters who was indifferent to the fate of his own works ; and the great original creator who borrowed at every turn from the writings of other men. Simpler views more easily reconciled with each other, and more consistent with ordinary experience, have been suggested in these pages.

II

STRATFORD-ON-AVON

There is a widely diffused belief, not confined to Baconian circles, that in the time of Shakespeare the inhabitants of Stratford were lost in ignorance, and could neither read nor write. But we have no ground for believing that Stratford was unique amongst English towns, and had sunk to depths beneath the familiar level of knowledge, that it was somehow more benighted than Coventry or Evesham, Worcester or Shrewsbury or Gloucester. And the mass of the nation in corporate boroughs, and even in villages and farms, cannot be lightly dismissed as illiterate.

It may even be argued that the rural population then possessed more intelligence than it does at the present time ; when centuries of migration to America and Australia, and to great industrial towns at home, have drained away the alert and enterprising individuals, leaving the residue to stagnation ; so that country life has lost its former character and forcefulness. Some such reflections are suggested by a comparison of Elizabeth's days with our own.

Conspicuous among the events of the sixteenth century

was the Reformation, which could only have taken place amongst men who were thoughtful and independent of judgment. And it drew some of its inspiration, as at the time was recognized, from the very poorest class. When Erasmus published his Greek Testament, he cast in the preface a wide view over society. He could not agree with those who were unwilling that laymen should read the Scriptures translated into the language of the people ; rather he preferred that the farmer should meditate upon them at the plough, that the weaver should have them in mind as he plied the shuttle, and the traveller beguile with their stories the tedium of the way. Thus Erasmus opened up free course for the Reformation in one of its channels, and rightly foresaw the eagerness with which the common folks would cast themselves into the study of the Bible. The triumph of the Reformation, basing, as it did, its principles on the first-hand knowledge of Scripture by laymen, would have been unintelligible, had education been limited to the very few.

" If God give me life, ere many years a boy that driveth the plough shall know more of the Scriptures than thou dost," was said by Tyndale to a priest. Surely these words suggest that ploughboys were able to read, and waited only for the opportunity ; and surely Tyndale knew more than we do about the age in which he lived. When the English Bible was being purchased everywhere, Parliament intervened with an Act, *Anno tricesimo quarto Henrici octavi*, founded upon curious class distinctions. The Chancellor of England, the King's Justices, noblemen and gentlemen, are permitted to read the Bible openly with their families in their houses and gardens. Merchants may read it in private to themselves ; but neither " artificers, prentices, journeymen, servingmen of the degree of yeomen and under, nor husbandmen, nor labourers shall read the Bible in English to themselves or any others, privately or openly." [1] The natural inference is that they were competent to do so ; for prohibition implies ability to do the thing prohibited. And the conclusion suggested by the Act is strengthened by detailed evidence. In the days when Protestantism passed through its last fiery trials, before its final victory, it was not bishops and divines alone who perished. Tradesmen, apprentices, weavers and fishermen were amongst the victims ; and all had studied the new interpretation of Scripture. A few amongst them could not read, and were influenced by the preaching and exhortation of others ; but these were rare exceptions. Foxe in his *Acts and Monuments* usually takes reading and writing for granted. Most of the Protestant sufferers, however humble their circumstances, pored over the Bible, had theological works in their possession, wrote letters and signed judicial depositions.

A book published at Oxford in 1546 has been found to contain this inscription by the purchaser :—

" When I kept Mr. Latimer's sheep, I bought this book, when the Testament was abrogated, that shepherds might not

---

[1] *Statutes of the Realm*, III, p. 896

read it. I pray God amend that blindness. Writ by Robert Williams, keeping sheep upon Sainbury Hill." [1]

Concerning the state of education under Elizabeth there is a mine of suggestion in Shakespeare himself. But it has not yet been carefully explored ; and the commons of England in his day have been casually identified with his Jack Cade in *Henry VI*. Cade is the uproarious enemy of all knowledge. He despises those who write their names : an honest and plain dealing man has only " a mark to himself." " Thou has caused printing to be used, and, contrary to the King, his crown and dignity, thou hast built a paper-mill," he says to Lord Say. The Clerk of Chartam is dragged in as a prisoner by Cade's followers. They have taken him " setting of boys' copies." " There's a villain ! " cries Cade, and orders the luckless clerk to be hanged with his pen and inkhorn about his neck.

This scene diverges very far from genuine history. There were two Peasant Risings, those of 1381 and 1450. On the first occasion the rioters did indeed " burn and destroy all records, evidences, court-rolls and other muniments,"—but their motive was not hostility to the written word itself. They wished to cancel old obligations, and to disorganize the collection of taxes. But when new charters of manumission were offered, they accepted them at once, and joyfully carried those treasures home. Moreover, they could and did read, and created a literature of their own. The chronicles of those times

[1] *Memoir of William Tyndale*, by George Offor, 1836, p. 89.

have preserved, in the original text, specimens of the manifestos which were written for the encouragement of the rebels and passed among them from hand to hand. Falsehood and guile, it was said, had reigned too long, and the commons must now make a good end of that they had begun,—for if the end be well, then all is well. Obviously, these curious documents were composed by the leaders to put heart and constancy into their followers ; but they would not have been written, if the peasants could not have read them.[1]

However, amongst men of different rank and calling strange tales sprang up, in the excitement and trepidation of the hour, and were carried by agitated fugitives to conventual places of refuge. A monk who sat listening and writing in the scriptorium of St. Albans heard terrible tales from the outer world. The rebels were determined to destroy all learning. It was dangerous to be recognized as a clerk, and still more dangerous if anyone were found with an inkhorn at his side,—" for such seldom or never escaped from them with life." [2]

Transferred to the pages of Holinshed, the wild rumour which had affrighted St. Albans Abbey in 1381 came to the knowledge of Shakespeare,—and in his brilliant and fantastic imagination gave birth to the scene in which the boisterous Jack Cade repudiates Grammar Schools and paper-mills, and hustles away the culprit who uses pen and ink. Men who despise learning and rejoice in

[1] Knighton's *Chronicon*, Rolls Series, p. 139.
[2] Walsingham's *Historia Anglicana*, Rolls Series, II, p. 9 ; Holinshed, 1586, p. 436.

their ignorance exist in every age, and Shakespeare, who did not love them, has carried their doctrine to its last extravagance. But historical truth is not always adjustable to comedy ; and the Jack Cade of the real world knew well how pen and ink should be employed. He presented a petition to the Government, asking for redress of grievances, and issued a safe-conduct to a London merchant under his own sign-manual,—documents which still exist in print.[1]

It is strange that whilst so much has been heard of the unreal Jack Cade, little attention has been given to other passages in Shakespeare which confute the assumption of general ignorance. When Prince Henry picked Falstaff's pocket, as he slept behind the arras, certain papers were found, tavern reckonings and memoranda, one of them being a bill for a capon and anchovies, five shillings and eightpence for sack, and a halfpenny for bread. Mrs. Quickly, the hostess, could make an intelligent use of the pen, and did not rely, as the tradesmen of Stratford are said to have done, on mechanical substitutes which dispensed with it altogether.

Winter's Tale presents other evidence, which carries us far from low life in London into the depths of the country, and shows, with poetical colouring, a rustic holiday in Warwickshire. The scene of the Fourth Act is at the cottage of a shepherd ; the country-folk are assembled, the clowns and rustic maidens. Autolycus, the pedlar, enters with his wares, which include printed ballads and notebooks. "I love a ballad in print," exclaims

[1] Stow's *Annales*, 1615, p. 388.

the shepherdess Mopsa; and eager hands quickly buy the sheets. The rustics do even more: the ballads are set to music, which they read at sight. " 'Tis in three parts," says Mopsa; and the clown will not stir till he has both tune and words.

In *Midsummer Night's Dream* appears a party of hempen homespuns, as they are called, rude mechanicals, hard-handed men, working for bread upon Athenian stalls,

" Which never laboured in their wits till now."

But their intent is to perform a play. Peter Quince, the carpenter, is the author of it; he has copied out the parts, and distributes them to the performers. " Have you the lion's part written," says Snug the joiner. " Pray you, if it be, give it me, for I am slow of study." They may all be slow of study, and their play may be a grotesque affair when performed before the ducal court of Athens; but at least a knowledge of reading and writing, possessed by all, has gone to the making of it.

Nor is this merely a fantasy of the poet's invention. It is a transcript from real life, made ridiculous enough, but a transcript none the less. For several centuries the popular amusement of English craftsmen was the performance of Miracle Plays in verse; their subjects were incidents in the Old and the New Testaments, the plays following each other in a series which might give entertainment for the whole of a summer's day. They were divided amongst the working-men, a separate play to each trade. Over the whole country, in every city and market town, such performances went on. But if those multitudes of rude mechanicals had been unable to read, they could never have studied their parts, and Miracle Plays would never have been heard of.

The taste for drama lingered long among the common people. Even so late as the middle of the seventeenth century a party of peasants in a country village in Oxfordshire combined to produce a comedy. The date was 1653 ; the play chosen was *Mucedorus*, a drama in blank verse which had once belonged to Shakespeare's company, and had been performed at Whitehall before James I, in which a King's son disguised as a shepherd, a King's daughter far from her father's court, a bear, a clown, and a wild man of the woods all act as their natures suggest. It was the country-folk of Stanton Harcourt who formed the dramatic company, and played the piece in their own village and in places round about.[1] A simple and Arcadian incident ; but impossible from the beginning if these peasants had been unable to read. That there was then more education in Stanton Harcourt than in Stratford is most improbable.

The Miracle Plays of an earlier time, as they have come down to us, are interspersed with Latin, the names of characters,—*Primus Pastor, Secundus Rex, Tertius Miles,*—and the stage directions being in the learned language. Those who wrote the plays and produced them had a knowledge of Latin which was familiar and facile, although it may not have been profound. There is nothing in this circumstance to cause astonishment. During the fifteenth and sixteenth centuries Latin was

[1] John Rowe, *Tragi-Comoedia*, 1653, *passim*.

to no small part of the English people as a second mother-tongue. Even in the depths of the country the bailiff who farmed an estate kept his accounts and made his report to the owner of the soil in Latin.[1] Town clerks used it for their minutes, lawyers for bonds and charters, and physicians for their case-books;—Dr. Hall of Stratford, the son-in-law of Shakespeare, set down the ailments of his patients and his treatment of them in Latin, for no eye but his own. Its use by professional scholars was universal. It was in Latin that More wrote his *Utopia*, and Camden his *History of England in the Reign of Elizabeth*. A stream of volumes came from the press in Latin, addressing a public which could read the language with as much facility as English itself. It was cultivated by dignified merchants, prosperous yeomen, and members of the feudal aristocracy. Scott, in his *Lay of the Last Minstrel*, depicts a Border nobleman, who leads an English army over the Scottish marches, and threatens the towers of Branksome—Lord William Howard, known to the rude borderers as Belted Will. In his castle at Naworth Belted Will had a library of Latin volumes, which he read diligently and with many annotations.[2]

The Universities were thronged with students drawn from every rank. Some were the sons of landed families, and city dignitaries ; some came from the poorest class, and were themselves so poor that by Act of Parliament

[1] Thorold Rogers, *Six Centuries of Work and Wages*, 1884, pp. 165, 166.

[2] Walsingham's *Historia Anglicana*, Rolls Series, p. x

scholars of Oxford and Cambridge were forbidden to beg on the high road, unless they had a licence to do so under the seal of the University.[1] But residence in College was by no means necessary to obtain a sound knowledge of Latin. The Grammar Schools provided an efficient training in the language, alike for those who afterwards proceeded to Oxford and Cambridge, and for the merchants and tradesmen, squires and farmers, who remained in their native place,—and for men of letters of the class arising under Elizabeth who were content with a Grammar School training and asked no more.

In the fifteenth and sixteenth centuries Grammar Schools were founded all over England, in country towns and even in large villages, by the zeal of merchants who had enriched themselves in trade, and were generous to the community. Amongst the schools thus endowed a prominent place may be given to that at Stratford-on-Avon. A school existed in the town, as episcopal registers show, as early as 1295. It was at first associated with the parish church; but when the new town of citizens and traders sprang up at a distance, and became prosperous, its inhabitants formed their Gild of the Holy Cross, an institution which included a school for the sons of its members. " If from this we inferred," says Mr. Leach, " that the burgesses of trading towns and their gilds vied with the churchmen in their interest in education, and insisted on having their Grammar Schools at their doors, the conclusion would be one which can be justified by evidence at our disposal from Boston and Grantham,

[1] *Statutes of the Realm*, III, p. 330.

from Ipswich and Wisbech." [1]   At first it was supported
solely by the Gild ; but in 1482 it was endowed by
Thomas Jolyffe, who bestowed upon the school his
lands in Stratford, upon condition that in future education should be free, the master " teaching all scholars
who come to him in the said town, and taking nothing
from his scholars for his teaching." The school was
refounded in 1553 ; the salary of the schoolmaster being
fixed at £20,—a large sum in the money of those days,
when the Provost of Eton received £30 a year, and
each of the masters £10. On more occasions than one
it was paid by John Shakespeare, the poet's father, when
acting as Chamberlain for the borough.

Such schools existed all over England in the time of
Elizabeth. Their number cannot have been less than 300.
An estimate of the number of pupils attending them is
afforded by some indications. The Latin Grammar then
used in England was that compiled by William Lyly,
which was officially authorized and had a monopoly.
The number of copies of it printed annually was at least
10,000, and in some years there was a supplementary
issue of 1,250 copies.[2] The sale indicates ten thousand
children beginning the study of Latin every year, but
not the total number attending the Grammar Schools,
which must have been very much greater.

Lists of the authors studied at Grammar Schools
have in some places survived to this day. At Saffron

---

[1] *Victoria History of Warwickshire*, II, p. 297.
[2] Foster Watson, *The English Grammar Schools to 1600*, p. 255.

Walden there are such documents, with the schoolmasters'
signatures,—the works to be read including Ovid's *Metamorphoses*, Sallust, the *Eclogues* and *Æneid* of Virgil,
Cicero's *Epistles*, Terence, Horace, and the *Copia Rerum
et Verborum* of Erasmus.[1] Latin composition, especially
"the making of epistles," was prescribed. But the
purpose in view was not so much a refined and scholarly
knowledge of Latin literature as an easy and familiar
grasp of the Latin language itself. With such a preparation all the authors lay open to the pupil's reading in
later life ; and he might apply the language every day
to more immediate purposes.

Latin was familiarly employed in the Stratford of
Shakespeare. It was the language of law, and although
English might be used in small transactions, nothing
but Latin was thought worthy of being engrossed on
parchment. Documents of the kind, some concerning
the property of John Shakespeare, still exist, and show
that in Stratford there were lawyers who could write
Latin fluently. A notion that the classical speech had
a greater permanence and dignity than English still
persisted, and suggested its employment also for monumental epitaphs. On the tomb of Shakespeare himself
in Stratford Church there is an inscription in Latin verse ;
another appears on the grave of Anne Hathaway, his wife ;
another commemorates their son-in-law, John Hall.
In the south transept is the tomb of Richard Hill, a
woollen draper of Stratford, and a friend of John Shakes-

---

[1] *Archæologia*, Vol. 34, p. 37.

peare, who died in 1593. It has inscriptions in four languages, English, Latin, Greek and Hebrew.[1]

That Latin was also the appropriate language of epistolary correspondence, unless when haste and brevity permitted a relapse into the vernacular, was another idea which had not quite gone out,—fostered as it was by the " making of epistles " at school. Few letters from the Stratford of that time have come down to us ;—most private letters have a very short lease of life, and we possess none of Shakespeare's own. But several exist which came into the hands of Richard Quiney, whose name is associated with that of Shakespeare himself. Quiney was a mercer and a member of the Corporation. In 1598 he was in London on the town's affairs, and resided at the Bell in Carter Lane near St. Paul's, where he composed a hurried note to Shakespeare, his " loving good friend and countryman." His business with the poet was urgent :

" I make bold of you as a friend, craving your help with £30 upon Mr. Bushell's and my security. You shall friend me much in helping me out of all the debts I owe in London, —I thank God—and much quiet my mind, which would not be indebted." [2]

---

[1] *Stratford Records*, II, p. 5.

[2] This letter was, it seems, never actually sent to Shakespeare, who may have anticipated its delivery by calling upon Quiney at his inn. Quiney carried it with him, amongst other papers, in his return to Stratford. He died a few years afterwards when in office as chief magistrate, and a number of documents, belonging to him, including the letter, were left among the municipal archives.

The tone of the letter, the request which it contains, and the evident feeling of the writer that his wishes will at once be complied with, indicate a very close intimacy between Quiney and Shakespeare. At a later date their families were connected by marriage, one of Quiney's sons becoming the husband of Shakespeare's daughter, Judith.

Quiney was a typical Stratford citizen of the time, a perfect example of the world in which Shakespeare was born and brought up, and to which by all the ties of early association he belonged.

During his stay in London he received several letters from home. There is one of them, which for a variety of reasons will be given in full :—

Patri suo amantissimo Mro. Richardo Quinye Richardus Quinye filius S.P.D.

Ego omni officio ac potius pietate erga te (mi pater) tibi gratias ago pro iis omnibus beneficiis quae in me contulisti ; te etiam oro et obsecro ut provideres fratri meo et mihi duos chartaceos libellos quibus maxime caremus hoc presenti tempore ; si enim eos haberemus, plurimus profecto iis usus esset nobis : et praeterea gratias tibi ago quia a teneris, quod aiunt, unguiculis, educasti me in sacrae doctrinae studiis usque ad hunc diem. Absit etiam verbulis meis vana adulationis suspicio, neque enim quenquam ex meis amicis cariorem aut amantiorem mei te esse judico ; et vehementer obsecro ut maneat semper egregius iste amor tuus sicut semper anteahac ; et quanquam ego non possum remunerare tua beneficia, omnem tamen ab intimis meis praecordiis tibi exoptabo salutem. Vale.

Filiolus tuus tibi obedientissimus,

RICHARDUS QUINYE.

The writer of this epistle, Richard Quiney the younger, was a boy of eleven when he composed these flowing periods. He has a simple request to make,—that his father will bring for himself and his brother two notebooks of which they have much need, and of which they will make good use : the rest is boyish devotion to a parent who was evidently kind and affectionate. It is probable that the letter was revised by the schoolmaster and that Richard afterwards made a fair copy. Such things were done in Grammar Schools every day. It may safely be believed that Shakespeare himself could compose an epistle as good as Richard's, when at the same tender age, and could read Latin as readily as Quiney, the mercer.

The elder Quiney had an intimate friend, Abraham Sturley, who had been settled for many years in Stratford. Sturley was a scholar of Cambridge, where his College was Queen's, had come into Warwickshire in the service of Sir Thomas Lucy, and was by profession a lawyer.[1] Several letters from Sturley to Quiney have escaped the accidents of time. He writes in 1598 from Stratford, after a journey, on business or pleasure, during which he has visited friends at Bedford and Cambridge, and has seen letters from Quiney himself to the same persons. He gives all the news of home, and much good counsel. The whole of one letter is in Latin, evidently dashed off with a flowing pen. Others are composed in a strange mixture of languages, passing from Latin to English and back again in alternate sentences, as if one were

[1] E. I. Fripp, *Master Richard Quyny*, 1924, p. 37.

as familiar as the other both to the writer and the recipient. Sturley mentions reading, and advises his friend to study Cicero's *Epistles*.

He was also well acquainted with Shakespeare, to whom he alludes several times in his correspondence. It is a precious survival, and does more than anything else to reveal the surroundings of the Stratford poet in his native place.   He was not lost there in mere Egyptian darkness.

The theory of illiteracy at Stratford was maintained, with much emphasis, by one of Shakespeare's biographers, Halliwell-Phillipps, whose presentation of the poet's history and environment has made him an unconscious but effective ally of the Baconian revolt.   He founded his doctrine on one fact alone, which at the first glance seems decisive.   In the records of the borough many of the Aldermen and Councillors signed by making a mark after their names ; and signatures to deeds were often attached in the same way.   Amongst those who thus subscribed was John Shakespeare, the poet's father.   He makes a mark both in the council records and private documents.   No example of his autograph has ever been found.

Making a mark is now so evident a sign of inability to write that the illiteracy attributed to John Shakespeare and many of his fellow-citizens was thought to be sufficiently established.

But the matter becomes less certain when more minutely examined.   The use of marks by our ancestors presents a difficult problem ; and the belief that it was a sign of ignorance is no longer confidently held. The cross used in making a signature was not, when first employed, a mere concession to the illiterate. It was the Holy Cross of the Christian Faith, and was drawn with the pen often by men who had the highest education of their time, as a solemn attestation by which they gave to their word a religious sanctity. It was so employed in early charters by Kings and noblemen, abbots and archbishops.[1]

Thus the cross, which is now " soiled with all ignoble use," and made a mere sign of vulgar ignorance, had at first no such associations. It had a higher value on a document than the written name; and it mattered little if the name was set down by a scribe, provided the signer added the cross with his own hand. The binding obligation was in the cross itself.

Other signs came into use,—trade-marks, monograms and fanciful devices by which an individual obtained " a mark to himself." The belief that there was nothing derogatory in signing with the cross, or with such symbols, lasted through the Middle Ages, and into the time of Elizabeth. Evidence from Stratford itself is not wanting. John Shakespeare had a next-door neighbour, Adrian Quiney, father of Richard Quiney, the poet's friend. Adrian Quiney could write very well and despatched several letters to his son when the latter was in London. He asks that the key of the study may be sent home, in order that he may seek there for certain documents, and talks garrulously of lambs, colts and knit hose at

[1] S. R. Maitland, *The Dark Ages*, 1844, p. 14; Thomas Madox, *Formulare Anglicanum*, 1702, p. xxvii.

Evesham market.[1] But in the records of Stratford Council, and on the very page where John Shakespeare makes a mark, Adrian Quiney also makes a mark.[2]

Even in more recent years, so late as the middle of the nineteenth century, persons who could have written their own signatures, had they thought fit to do so, frequently made a mark like Adrian Quiney. Lord Campbell stated in 1859, after a lifetime spent in the practice of the law, that in his own experience he had seen many documents bearing a mark as the signature of persons who could write well.[3] The usage was even recognized by a decision of the Court of Queen's Bench. Having to choose between two wills made by the same individual, of which one was signed with a mark and the other in the testator's handwriting, the Court unanimously sustained the former, on the ground that, when the law gave to every one permission to use a mark, it did not inquire whether he was able to write or not.[4]

It is very improbable that the merchants of Stratford were lost in illiteracy. A man who cannot wield the pen may be a bricklayer or a ploughman ; but commerce cannot be carried on without some kind of book-keeping. And in this matter there is no invincible ignorance. The inconveniences that arise from lack of ability to write may be overcome by the simple expedient of acquiring it,— which any intelligent man can accomplish in a very brief

[1] Fripp, *Master Richard Quyny*, pp. 144, 145, 179.
[2] Savage and Fripp, *Stratford-upon-Avon Records*, V, p. 134.
[3] *Shakespeare's Legal Acquirements*, p. 15.
[4] *Revised Reports*, Pollock, Vol. 47, p. 502.

space of time. What was done in its absence? The usual but vague explanation hints at "tallies"; but the answer does not remove the difficulty. Tallies were pieces of smooth wood used in keeping accounts, on which sums were indicated by cutting notches on the edge. But they also bore inscriptions in writing, which stated the name of the debtor, and the nature of the debt; and without such inscription they would have been merely useless. Their common employment can be easily accounted for; wood being cheaper and more plentiful than paper.[1] In Scott's *Antiquary*, the baker's wife made use of " nick-sticks," or tallies, in her business; but she could, and did read the private letters of other people which fell into her hands.

Besides his private activities, John Shakespeare was a member of the Common Council, and for several years he acted as one of the Chamberlains, or treasurers of the borough, receiving the public funds and making disbursements. In January, 1564, the Town Clerk put on record the financial statement of John Taylor and John Shakespeare for the preceding twelvemonth, which contains entries of *Money Received*, sixteen items; *Money paid upon Receipt*, thirty-five items, including sums for such things as locks and keys, new bell-ropes, sawing timber; and *Allowances*, nine items, including fees paid to the Chamberlains themselves for their services. There follows the declaration that " John Taylor and John

---

[1] Hilary Jenkinson, *Exchequer Tallies, Archæologia*, 1911, where illustrations of tallies are given, showing the writing upon them.

Shakespeare have made a true and lawful account for their time being Chamberlains, *et sic quieti sunt*.[1]

The natural inference from these words is that Taylor and Shakespeare had themselves kept the notes of receipt and expenditure in a methodical fashion ; and that the Town Clerk had done no more than copy out their jottings in an official hand, with a little Latin embellishment.

Halliwell-Phillipps, however, suggests a picture, which must surely be imaginary, of a John Shakespeare who is unacquainted with penmanship. " Nearly all tradesmen then reckoned with counters," it is said ; and John Shakespeare is described as an adept in this art ; but how a counter could be used to designate a lock or a bell-rope is not quite clear. Such things might be an aid to arithmetic, but could not be a substitute for writing, when records had to be kept. Sometimes also, it is added, illiterate tradesmen resorted to " professional scriveners." Now we begin to see light. John Shakespeare buys for the public use a bell-rope, or a door, and hastens to a scrivener in the next street to have the purchase and price entered in his notebook. In the year 1563 the number of these visits to the penman must have amounted to exactly sixty. He also makes payment upon receipt, obtaining for each a written acknowledgment, which to him is an unintelligible scrap of paper, and hurries to the scrivener, to find out whether it is in order or not. There is no mention in the accounts

[1] Savage and Fripp, *Stratford-upon-Avon Records*, I, p. 129.

themselves of anything paid for such assistance in keeping them.

To augment our surprise, we learn that John Shakespeare's services did not cease with his own demission of office as Chamberlain. For the following year William Tyler and William Smith were elected ; but these gentlemen were content to leave the performance of the duties to their two predecessors. When the time came to render up their trust, the Town Clerk made this entry in his minutes,—" The account of William Tyler and William Smith, Chamberlains, made by John Shakespeare and John Taylor." We can but believe that these words tell the literal truth, and that Shakespeare and Taylor actually set down their financial statement in their own writing. When the copy in the Council minutes had been duly engrossed, there was no need to preserve the original.

The theory of John Shakespeare's illiteracy cannot be saved by suggesting that his colleague may have possessed some education and wielded the pen for both. In Council minutes where John Shakespeare signs by making a mark, John Taylor does so also. If mark-making be a sign of illiteracy, they are both in the same condemnation.

Nor can the matter be explained by supposing that the Town Clerk himself kept the accounts, and attributed them to the Chamberlains as a mere official formality. Such a theory would not harmonize with his conduct on the second occasion, when he speaks of the account " made by John Shakespeare and John Taylor," although they are now out of office, instead of assigning it to the actual Chamberlains, their successors, to whom a merely nominal honour would have belonged. The conclusion is irresistible that when we read the Stratford accounts for 1563 and 1564, we are in the presence of the only compositions by the poet's father which have been preserved, but his genuine works none the less.

When he denied writing to the family and early friends of Shakespeare,—and thus, all unwittingly, laid the foundation on which the Baconians were afterwards to rear their edifice—Halliwell-Phillipps denied also the possibility and means of reading. The young Shakespeare, he tells us, was brought up amongst " illiterate relatives in a bookless neighbourhood." To prove the existence of many books in the Stratford of Elizabeth is now impossible. Evidence about the property of former ages is chiefly derived from legal documents in which books are seldom mentioned. But some fragments of information can here and there be gleaned. Philip Rogers, an apothecary, raised an action against Valentine Palmer to recover a book on Surgery which he had lent him. Rogers used the book for professional purposes, but Palmer wished to read it, for entertainment or instruction, or he would not have borrowed it. Margaret Young brought a suit against Joan Parrett to recover some property which had come into the possession of the latter, and of which Margaret Young claimed to be the rightful owner. The articles in dispute included three prayer books, and another volume which had already been disposed of by Joan Parrett, and had passed into the possession of—

" Mr. Shakespeare." The date was 1595. At that time William Shakespeare had been long in London, and had not yet acquired a house in Stratford and settled again in his native place. The person who was naturally spoken of then in Stratford as " Mr. Shakespeare " was John Shakespeare, the father.

Halliwell-Phillipps himself, when exploring the Corporation archives, came upon some detached sheets which had formed part of Frobisher's *Discovery of Cataya*, published in black-letter in 1578.

Other evidence of an interesting kind appears in the will of the Rev. John Bretchgirdle, Vicar of Stratford, who held that position in 1564, and stood at the font when the infant William Shakespeare was baptized.

Mr. Bretchgirdle had an extensive library, in Latin, Greek and English, and bestowed a great part of it in legacies, especially remembering his godsons and other youthful friends. To one of them he left his copies of Virgil and Horace, to another the works of Josephus, and to another the *Encheiridion* of Erasmus. During his residence in Stratford, he had lived on terms of special friendship with one of his parishioners, William Smith, a linen-draper, and a member of the Common Council. Mr. Smith had several sons, to each of whom the Vicar left a token of his affection ; his bequests to them including versions of the *Psalms* and the *Acts of the Apostles* in English, Æsop's *Fables* and Sallust in Latin. It may be believed that he expected his young friends to make good use of the books which he bestowed upon

D

them ; and there is no reason to suppose that the sons
of Alderman Smith had an advantage in early training
over contemporary boys in Stratford.

That boys received a more complete education than
girls may be readily allowed ; but Shakespeare generally
assumes that women were at least able to read and write.
In *Love's Labour's Lost* the pedantic schoolmaster of the
parish, Holofernes, bristling with Latin, is followed
everywhere by the curate Sir Nathaniel ; who thus
expresses his admiration : " Sir, I praise the Lord for
you, and so may my parishioners ; for their sons are
well tutored by you, and their daughters profit very
greatly under you : you are a good member of the
commonwealth." In *Midsummer Night's Dream* Helena
says of Hermia,—" She was a vixen, when she went to
school " ; and Maria in *Twelfth Night*, although only a
waiting-maid, can write so good a hand that it is indis-
tinguishable from that of the Countess Olivia, and composes the letter which deceives Malvolio. Behind these
passages is plainly visible a world where women were
not without cultivation.

Education was then, if not universal, at least a very
common thing in Shakespeare's Stratford. Nor was it,
as has too often been suggested, a mere country village,
inhabited by a rustic populace. It was a small metro-
polis for the district round, and stood higher in relative
size and rank among English towns than it does at the
present day. It had prospered in trade, in spite of
inevitable fluctuations, and had a community of successful
middle-class people, as well as several landowning

families, who resided there for convenience, society and the education of their children. Some of its citizens combined both qualities ; they carried on trade or manufacturing, and also held land of their own, of which they supervised the cultivation. A certain Robert Perrott, traceable in sundry documents, was a brewer, owned the manor of Luscombe, some five or six miles away, and Richard Woodward, gentleman, also resided at Stratford, and derived his income from the manor of Quinton in Gloucestershire. In the Public Record Office may be seen a little manuscript, neatly written in a clerkly hand, and entitled *A Book of the Names of the Gentlemen and Freeholders in the county of Warwick.* Its date is 1580. The names entered in the list for Stratford-on-Avon amount to thirty-eight, of which the sixth in order is that of John Shakespeare.

The mark of a certain social distinction was the possession of a coat-of-arms, to which a greater importance was given then than now. Public officials, the Heralds, supervised the use of arms ; they compiled lists of families entitled to bear them and recorded their descent ; considered applications for a grant, and took drastic steps to exclude unauthorized claimants. From time to time the Heralds made a visitation of England, passing through each county in turn ; they called before them all persons who used coat-armour, examined their pedigrees and shields ; and put them on record. Sometimes they even compiled a black list of persons purporting to bear arms who had been disqualified, and were warned to desist. On some occasions arms unlawfully used and placed on monuments were publicly defaced by the Heralds with hammers.

The right to bear arms was then the official recognition, made after due inquiry, of a certain rank and consideration in society ; it carried with it the title of " gentleman " to which those without arms had no claim. In the Heralds' *Visitation of Warwickshire*, compiled in 1619, we find a group of such families residing in Stratford,—those of Clopton, Underhill, Trussell, Woodward, Nash, Reynolds, Combe, Lane and Kempton. It was amongst such people that Shakespeare was born and bred, and found his Stratford friends and associates ; several of their names occur in his will.

Natives of Stratford found their way to success in other regions ; through the Universities or by business aptitude : the notion of Stratford as a closed circle of narrow minds and unenterprising spirits is altogether misleading.

Examples may be found of Stratford lads going out into the world and meeting with prosperity enough. Richard Field, son of a tanner, whose father was a friend of the elder Shakespeare, settled in London as a printer and publisher : the first editions of *Venus and Adonis* and *Lucrece* came from his press. The younger Richard Quiney, author of the Latin epistle, became a merchant in London, and at his death left houses and lands, a part share in a shop called the *Seven Sisters*, and a plantation in Virginia. John Sadler, his cousin, also became a merchant in London, and combined with Quiney to present two silver maces to the Corporation of Stratford ; he also left lands and houses and a plantation in Virginia. Another native of the place, John Lane, made voyages as a merchant in the Levant, and left a will which he had written at Famagusta in the island of Cyprus, having taken a passage for England in the ship *Unicorn*, and fearing he might not survive the voyage. John Lane had gathered Spanish pieces of eight to the value of £800 in English money, which he bequeathed to his mother, Katherine Lane of Stratford-on-Avon, and his brother then apprenticed in London. William Smith of Stratford found his way to Moscow, and was employed at the court of the Czar. Like a true Englishman of his time, he afterwards wrote to the Heralds in London to ask for a coat-of-arms, describing himself as " servant to the Emperor's Majesty of Russia," and pleading his father's position as an Alderman and his relationship to the Bishop of Winchester. His letter may be seen in the British Museum.[1]

Stratford had its own full share in the spirit of enterprise of which Shakespeare speaks on the first page of one of the first comedies he wrote :—

> " Homekeeping youths have ever homely wits.
> I rather would entreat thy company
> To see the wonders of the world abroad,
> Than, living dully sluggardiz'd at home,
> Wear out thy youth with shapeless idleness."

Shakespeare himself was inspired by the restless eagerness which was abroad in his time : it was that and no

[1] Harleian MS., 1471, f. 98.

external circumstances, which first took him from Stratford to London. And the young men of Stratford left
it like him, to seek preferment out,—

> " Some to the wars, to try their fortunes there ;
>   Some to discover islands far away ;
>   Some to the studious Universities,"

carried from their native haunts, as Shakespeare has
said in another of his earliest plays, by

> " Such wind as scatters young men through the world
>   To seek their fortune further than at home,
>   Where small experience grows."

It is not without significance that such passages occur
in Shakespeare's most youthful works.

The town itself was a pleasant place of abode for those
who remained, or, like Shakespeare, returned in later
life. Stratford has not so much changed in three hundred
years that we cannot now recognize the features it had
in the days of Elizabeth. The river Avon, flowing
through its meadows in a graceful curve, is still crossed
by the long stone bridge which Sir Hugh Clopton, a
wealthy merchant and Lord Mayor of London, presented
to his native place, many years before Shakespeare was
born. On its bank is the church of the Holy Trinity,
with its slender spire ; and the chapel of the Holy Cross,
a beautiful piece of late Gothic, stands beside the spacious
and still delightful garden where Shakespeare walked on
summer days. The streets are interspersed with plain
houses in the modern taste, or lack of it ; but many
Elizabethan dwellings survive, with their half-timbered

fronts, carved beams, and pointed gables : larger houses
of equal age stand in the outskirts of the town among
gardens, with their lines of bay windows and porches
adorned with armorial shields. No one who contemplates
these Tudor dwellings, and compares them with the
ugly structures of more recent date which diversify the
place, could ever conclude that the moderns may despise
the Stratford Elizabethans on æsthetic grounds.

Where architecture fails, drainage may succeed ; and
the Baconians enlarge, with a curious insistence, on the
insanitary condition of the place. But there is no
cause for believing that Stratford was more neglected
than any other English town in the same period ; and its
sanitation was infinitely better than that of London,
with its crowded and narrow streets, open channels,
dreadful odours, and ever-threatening plague,—a city
" Where houses thick and sewers annoy the air," as
Milton has described it. With infinite solace he escaped
from London " to breathe among the pleasant villages
and farms,"—as Shakespeare had done before him.

Several travellers visited Stratford and put their impressions on record. William Camden, in his *Britannia*,
has described it as a handsome market town—*non in-
elegans* is his own expression,—which had given birth to
John of Stratford, an Archbishop of Canterbury, and to
Clopton, Lord Mayor of London. Camden published
his work in 1586, when a greater son of Stratford was
still unknown to the world. At an earlier date John
Leland passed through the place, and jotted down some
remarks :—

" There is a right goodly chapel in a fair street towards the south end of the town, newly re-edified in mind of man by one Hugh Clopton, Mayor of London, . . . This Hugh Clopton builded also by the north side of this chapel a pretty house of brick and timber, wherein he lay in his latter days and died."

Stratford was thus chosen for the rural retirement of a Lord Mayor as well as of a poet. And the pretty house of brick and timber which he built in the fair street has another claim on our notice. It was also the house in which Shakespeare himself passed his later days and died. The manner of life which was once led by the inhabitants of its picturesque dwellings need not be a sealed book to us : it is a very open book if we will but turn its pages and read. All is revealed in *The Merry Wives of Windsor*, which might with equal propriety have been called *The Merry Wives of Stratford*. Mr. Ford and Mr. Page are such men as managed their warehouses and cultivated their land on the bank of the Avon, three hundred years ago. Justice Shallow and his cousin Slender came in from the country to visit their town acquaintance, and to dine with Page on venison which Shallow has already presented to his host. Page himself has rural tastes, likes a day's sport, has his hawks and hounds. Mrs. Ford and Mrs. Page are far from unintelligent and have no difficulty in reading the amorous letters of Sir John Falstaff, the fat and now foolish knight. Anne Page has seven hundred pounds left her by her grandfather, which, with expectations, is accounted good gifts. Little William Page attends the Grammar School, like little Richard Quiney, and his father complains that he profits nothing in the world at his book. Mr. Page may not know Latin as well as Mr. Quiney and Mr. Sturley ; but, being a sensible man, he does not express an opinion without having the means of forming it. But Hugh Evans the schoolmaster, at the mother's request, puts William through some questions on his accidence, and he is found a better scholar than he was thought to be ; he has a good sprag memory. The world is all before William Page ; he may proceed from the Grammar School to Oxford ; he may in time be a poet, or a Bishop. We do not find Page and Ford with books in their hands ; perhaps they did not read a great deal ; but Slender, the foolish young squire, who swears by his gloves, which were made by Alderman Shakespeare, has his *Book of Songs and Sonnets*, of which he is inordinately fond, and his *Book of Riddles*, which he has lent to Alice Shortcake ; and Alice Shortcake can read it, or why should she want it ? Even Bardolph, the coney-catching rascal, who picks Master Slender's pocket, was at school in his time, and can call up some scraps of Latin in moments of inspiration. Such are the figures which pass and re-pass in Stratford, here called Windsor.

III

FAMILY HISTORY

John Shakespeare, father of the poet, was not himself a native of Stratford, but came of land-holding and farming stock, the sound old class of yeomanry, which was believed to be the strength of the nation and the mettle of its pasture. His father, Richard Shakespeare, was tenant of a farm at Snitterfield, on the heights which rise to the north of the town. Further back modern research has not been able to trace the Shakespeares. Their name was a common one in Warwickshire, —so common that John Shakespeare has sometimes been confused with another John, and behind William Shakespeare we may see the pale shadow of William Shakespeare who dealt in malt.

When a young man, John Shakespeare moved from Snitterfield to Stratford, and engaged in business there, as a glover or white-tawer. The white-tawer,—from whose designation comes the family name *Whittier*,— prepared the softer kinds of leather, sheepskin, deerskin and kid ; from which were manufactured many kinds of goods,—gloves, girdles, collars, caps, laces, purses and parchment. This is a sufficient account of John Shakespeare's activities as a craftsman, and indicates enough to employ his skill and fill his warehouse. The statement that he was " a considerable dealer in wool " was made more than a century after his decease by Nicholas Rowe, in his brief and often inaccurate life of the poet. Rowe cites no authority ; and his assertion is plainly irreconcilable with the evidence of contemporary documents. He was probably aware of the fact that dealing in wool was once a common and profitable trade in the Midland Counties, and hastily concluded from the general to the particular.

The wife of John Shakespeare was Mary Arden, daughter of Robert Arden, a prosperous farmer residing at Wilmecote, a few miles from Stratford. The name and descent of Robert Arden have much occupied the biographers of Shakespeare. He belonged to a younger branch of one of the most ancient families in England. The pedigree of the Ardens fills many pages in the *Visitation of Warwickshire ;* and their history is related by the learned antiquary, Sir William Dugdale. They were older than the Norman Conquest, their founder being a Saxon nobleman, Turchill, who resided at Warwick and held great possessions in the county. Turchill had the good fortune to escape the confiscation which followed the battle of Hastings, and was received into favour by William the Conqueror. His name appears in Domesday Book, and the lands ascribed to him there were extensive. He was one of the first of the Saxons to follow the Norman custom of using a surname, and adopted that of Arden, the name then given to his native district. His descendants continued to hold a place of eminence among the gentry of Warwickshire, and for several centuries had their chief seat at Park Hall near Birmingham. Their names appear in English history in times of war and civil commotion, and more than once they found themselves on the losing side, threatened with the penalty of attainder. In the time of Henry III, Sir Thomas Arden took part with the barons who had risen against the king under Simon de Montfort. He was taken prisoner when his party was defeated at Evesham, and could only ransom himself by the sacrifice of his lands. But the family fortunes revived, and the lands were recovered. Two hundred years later another Civil War broke out and again the Ardens were in peril. Robert Arden of Park Hall adopted the cause of the White Rose. He fell into the hands of the Lancastrians, and was tried for high treason and beheaded at Ludlow in 1452. His property was confiscated. But with the rising of the sun of York prosperity returned to the ancient house. Its estates were restored by Edward IV to Walter Arden, son of the unfortunate Robert, and a new period in its history began.

Park Hall, the seat of the Ardens, passed long ago into other hands ; in the main line they are extinct ; and their lineage and alliances have become little more than a matter of genealogical history, to which their connection with Shakespeare has directed modern research.

Walter Arden, who recovered the estates under Edward IV, married Eleanor Hampden, daughter of John Hampden, an ancestor of the statesman who led the opposition to Charles I in the Long Parliament, and was mortally wounded at Chalgrove Field. There were several sons of the marriage. John Arden, the eldest, inherited Park Hall and the family estates. A few surviving documents afford some glimpses of this Tudor Squire. He was in service at Court as Esquire of the Body to Henry VII ; and in his will he mentions a room in his house known as the King's Chamber, which is suggestive of royal visits. His suit of white armour he left to adorn a figure of St. George to be placed in the parish church. The will also shows the homeliness which was mingled with Tudor dignity, and the testator's very practical interest in agriculture. Bequests were made to the church and to relatives in the form of horses, oxen and heifers, and stated quantities of rye, oats, wheat and barley.

Our concern is rather with a younger brother of this gentleman, Thomas Arden, from whom Shakespeare himself was descended. Thomas Arden settled at Wilmecote, near Stratford, acquired land there and in the neighbouring village of Snitterfield, and spent a long life as a farmer on his own ground. He was succeeded in the property by his son, Robert Arden ; who was the father of Mary Arden, the wife of John Shakespeare, and mother of the poet.

When stated in this form, the story is clear and simple ; but it has been pieced together by a difficult process of research ; and objections to it are made by some Shakespearian scholars. They admit that John Arden of Park Hall had a younger brother called Thomas ; they admit also that a Thomas Arden resided for many years at Wilmecote, and was certainly the great-grandfather of the poet, but they dispute their identification, and contend for two men of the same name, of whom the first had his home in some unknown place, and the second came of a different and humble stock.

In favour of the belief that we are dealing with no more than one individual, who was both the younger brother of John Arden and the poet's ancestor, is the fact that Shakespeare himself claimed descent from the house of Arden and the right to bear its arms. The connection also was allowed by the Heralds, who described his grandfather, Robert Arden, as a " gentleman of worship." That both Shakespeare and the Heralds acted in good faith must be admitted, unless sufficient reason can be shown to the contrary. On the other side is an argument of a general nature, which in itself is far from conclusive. Thomas Arden of Wilmecote is dismissed as a mere farmer or husbandman whose inferior station in life makes it impossible that he could be allied to a family of such wealth and dignity. He was only a humble namesake, a mere tiller of the soil.

But those who advance this argument forget that he was poorer than his elder brother by inevitable circumstances. The lot of younger sons was proverbially a hard one. Both law and practice combined to keep the estate unbroken, from one generation to another, in the hands of the eldest son and heir, for the maintenance and perpetuation of the family name. Younger sons had to accept what provision could be made for them, to engage in agriculture or business, or to sink into the class of mere adventurers. Shakespeare himself has sufficiently illustrated their position. Orlando in *As You Like It* has an elder brother, whose title in blood is no better than his own ; he has, however, inherited from his father but a poor thousand crowns, is kept rustically at home, fed with hinds, and trained like a peasant. Edward Poins in *Henry IV* is the second son of a good house ; but, although he associates almost on equal terms with the Prince of Wales, he has no visible resources and hangs loosely on society.

Appeals to elder brothers for financial assistance, and actions against them to recover small sums of money, were common, and were not unknown in the Arden family itself. John Arden, the King's Esquire, had several brothers, of whom Henry was the youngest. In the records of the Court of Chancery is a bill presented by Henry Arden against John, in which he asks for payment of a meagre allowance made by their father, and appeals for the commiseration of the court on the ground that John has great possessions of lands and great substance of goods, whilst he himself, being only a younger brother, has but little to live upon.[1]

Thomas Arden of Wilmecote was in much more flourishing circumstances than this luckless Henry, who was, beyond dispute, a member of the Park Hall family, with all its claims to long descent and armorial bearings ; and his farming is not enough to debar him from a connection with that ancient line. John Arden himself,

[1] Early Chancery Proceedings, Bundle 461, No. 29.

with his bequests of horses, oxen and heifers, rye, oats, wheat and barley, would not have refused to acknowledge Thomas as a brother on the ground of his agricultural pursuits. Moreover, a direct connection between the husbandman of Wilmecote and the main branch of the family is established by a common friendship of an interesting and significant kind. When Walter Arden made a settlement upon his wife, he formed a body of trustees to whom certain property was conveyed by a legal instrument for the purpose.[1]

The most prominent among them was Sir Robert Throckmorton, a gentleman of dignified rank in Warwickshire, and who died at Rome when on a pilgrimage to the Holy Land. The same Sir Robert Throckmorton gave his services in a similar capacity to Thomas Arden of Wilmecote. When the latter purchased his estate in Snitterfield, he executed a deed by which several of his friends were associated with him in the transaction ; and the first name in the list is that of Sir Robert Throckmorton. The next is that of Thomas Trussell of Billingsley, a man of good birth and rank, who was Sheriff of Warwick and Leicester in 1508. It is plain that Thomas Arden of Wilmecote, Shakespeare's ancestor, was accustomed to move in the best society which Warwickshire could afford.

His own means provided him with comfort, if not ostentation. He had at Wilmecote a farm called Asbies, to which about sixty acres of land were attached, and houses and gardens in Snitterfield, with about a hundred

[1] Early Chancery Proceedings, Bundle 278, No. 70.

acres more. The property descended at his death to his
son, Robert Arden, Shakespeare's grandfather. There
was no son to succeed him in his turn ; but he had several
daughters, of whom Mary Arden was the youngest and
evidently the favourite. It was to her that the farm of
Asbies with its sixty acres was bequeathed. In due course
it would have descended to Shakespeare himself, but
before the death of his parents it had passed out of their
hands by mortgage, and was never recovered.

With the profit of his business as a glover and the sub-
stantial inheritance of his wife, John Shakespeare seems
to have begun in prosperity. He became one of the
most prominent citizens of Stratford ; acted, as we have
seen, as one of the Chamberlains who managed the finances
of the borough ; wore the gown of an Alderman ; and
entered upon his year of office as Bailiff, a title equivalent
to Mayor, in 1568. He acquired property in the town,
including the house in Henley Street, which is still
preserved, and is shown as the birthplace of his son.

But, as he is traced through the records of Stratford,
a cloud afterwards seems to come over John Shakespeare ;
there are legal proceedings and debts ; a John Shakespeare is mentioned who has been sued for money due,
but is reported to have nothing on which it is possible
to distrain. It is the common opinion that his business
declined and he sank into poverty. But the matter is
complicated by the fact that there was then in Stratford
another and less notable John Shakespeare, a younger
man described as a shoemaker, who has been more than
once confused with his namesake : to make a distinct

separation between allusions to one and to the other is a perplexing task. It is possible that it was actually the shoemaker who had nothing which could be distrained upon. His phantom haunts the background of the story ; and no one has yet succeeded in driving it away.

Certain entries in the Corporation accounts have been quoted as further indications that Alderman Shakespeare was a man in embarrassed circumstances ; but their evidence also is uncertain. In an assessment levied for the relief of the poor in 1578, it is stated that each Alderman shall pay fourpence,—" saving John Shakespeare and Robert Bratt who shall not be taxed to pay anything." That both were unable to pay is the usual assumption. But in another assessment made in the same year, Alderman Bratt is once more discharged ; he is to pay " nothing in this place." Now this place is Stratford ; and it is natural to infer that Alderman Bratt is living elsewhere, beyond the boundary of the town, and making payment in another parish. John Shakespeare also may have resided at that time outside the borough, and for that reason may have been exempted or lightly rated in Stratford itself.

But at least one serious misfortune undoubtedly befell John Shakespeare. Two years after the fourpenny affair just mentioned, he found himself confronted by a much more formidable demand. He was summoned, under circumstances which are mysterious enough, to present himself before the Court of Queen's Bench at Westminster ; he failed to do so, and was heavily fined. In the *Coram Rege Roll* for 1580 the story is recorded.

John Shakespeare of Stratford-on-Avon, yeoman, had not appeared on a certain day, to give sufficient security that he would keep the Queen's peace, and the fine imposed upon him amounted to £20. Two friends had given security to produce John Shakespeare at the appointed time; they also were in default and were fined £10 each. They were John Audley of Nottingham and Thomas Cooby of Stoke-on-Trent.

The next entry on the parchment continues the same tale. John Audley of Nottingham had also been summoned before the Court of Queen's Bench to give security that he would be of good behaviour; he also failed to appear; and was very severely dealt with. The court doubled the fine, and amerced John Audley in the sum of £40. Two friends had given security for his appearance; they also were fined, and again the fines were doubled and became £20 apiece. The securities for John Audley were Thomas Cooby of Stoke-on-Trent and John Shakespeare of Stratford-on-Avon. It is not the least of Mrs. Stopes's services to Shakespearian investigation that she was the discoverer of this important document.

This is the most signal and astonishing incident in the otherwise uneventful life of the poet's father, and throws upon it a flood of light. It is clear that the Court of Queen's Bench regarded John Shakespeare as a man of substance and position. £40, the total amount of his fines, was a very large sum in the money of those days. Such fines, which the court must have intended to be heavy but not unpayable, were imposed on the man whom his brother Aldermen had lately exempted from an assessment of fourpence, because—according to the usual interpretation—he had not fourpence in his pocket.

But, it must be inquired, what had John Shakespeare and John Audley actually done to bring down the terrors of the law in this fashion upon their heads. They were asked to give security that they would be of good behaviour and would preserve the Queen's peace. That they had been guilty of some disorderly and illegal act is apparent ; but its nature can only be conjectured. From the legal expressions employed, taken in conjunction with the circumstances of the time, we may believe that adherence to Catholicism would adequately explain the affair.

Although Protestantism had become the official religion under Elizabeth, the Catholics had not lost hope of a restoration, and the Protestants did not feel themselves to be firmly and permanently established. The aim of the Government was uniformity in religion,—no other method was then understood,—and uniformity was to be obtained by the suppression of Catholicism in every part of the country. The policy of Elizabeth's ministers was directed steadily to that end, and succeeded in reducing the Catholics to impotence ; aided as it was by an even more potent cause,—the association between the Papacy and the foreign enemies of England, especially the threatening power of Spain, which rallied public feeling to the Protestant side.

By the middle of Elizabeth's reign the resolute Catholics who were ready to endure all things for their cause had become a small and harried minority ; but there were still many waverers who accepted the new faith with reluctance, and would have adhered to the old, if they could have done so without opposition to the law. They attended the parish churches as seldom as possible, heard Mass if an opportunity presented itself, associated in private with those who were like-minded with themselves, and regretted the age of change and unsettlement in which their lot was cast.

No clear-cut distinction had yet been drawn between Catholic and Protestant ; and many men who were willing to accept the Sovereign as head of the Church still clung with affection to the old rites with which they had been familiar from childhood. They were perplexed and inconsistent, sometimes they took the oath of supremacy, and complied with new ecclesiastical ordinances. Sometimes the spirit of Dissent revived. On several occasions, when the extreme Catholics themselves had plunged into dangerous and treasonable practices, the work of repression was carried on with peculiar energy and comprehensiveness. One of those outbursts of severity took place in 1580,—the year in which John Shakespeare was summoned before the Court of Queen's Bench. Multitudes of Catholics in every part of the country were then being sought out, arrested and imprisoned, and subjected to heavy fines.

But the Government was unwilling to represent these proceedings as religious persecution, and tried to give them a purely civil character. Recusants were not proceeded against for their faith, but for illegal and disloyal acts. It was the duty of every good and peaceful subject to be regular in his attendance at church, as the law required. Abstention from service, and presence at Catholic ceremonies, which by statute was forbidden, were considered as disorderly conduct, calculated to disturb the peace and security of the realm ; and recusants were summoned before the courts and bound over to be of good behaviour, under heavy penalties.

This method of dealing with Catholic recusants involved something which might justly be called a legal fiction ; but it was deliberately adopted and maintained by the authorities ; and it is sufficiently illustrated by cases recorded in the Acts of the Privy Council. Having heard that in Lincolnshire " divers persons not only forbear to come to their parish churches, but also secretly have used other Popish service " the Privy Council commanded that " all such disorders " should be punished and reformed according to the laws. A Catholic, named Bowewater, had been arrested, and showed some sign of willingness to conform ; and it was decided that he should be released after giving " bonds and sureties of him to Her Majesty's use for good behaviour for the space of one year following." Another Catholic, called Robert Blaydes, had been committed to the Tower, and on his submission orders were given for his release " either upon sureties or his own bonds for his good behaviour." These causes occurred in 1579, the year before the prosecution of John Shakespeare and John Audley, in which similar expressions were employed.

In 1581 this procedure was consolidated by a statute

entitled, " An Act to retain the Queen's Majesty's Subjects in their due Obedience " ; by which it was provided that all persons who did not repair to some church or chapel for common prayer should be heavily fined, and, after certificate in writing made to the Court of Queen's Bench, should be " bound with two sufficient sureties in the sum of two hundred pounds at least to their good behaviour." Elizabeth's lawyers left it in no doubt that even a silent abstention from church-going could be construed as an act detrimental to the peace of the Queen and her lieges.

The weapon which had thus been forged and polished was not allowed to lie idle. Under Elizabeth it was used against the Catholics. Under Charles II it was brought forth once more from the armoury, and turned against Puritan divines and their congregations. Richard Baxter relates that in 1684 he was arrested, with about a thousand others, who were all brought before the sessions and bound over to be of good behaviour, Baxter himself to find sureties to the amount of £400.

" I desired," he says, " to know what my crime was, and who were my accusers ; but they told me it was for no fault, but to secure the government in evil times. . . . I told them I had rather they would send me to jail than put me to wrong others, by being bound with me in bonds that I was likely to break to-morrow ; for if there did but five persons come to where I was praying, they could take it for a breach of good behaviour,"—

the presence of five persons at such an assembly being enough to make it an illegal meeting, and to justify the authorities in forfeiting Baxter's security.

It is probable that John Shakespeare, John Audley and Thomas Cooby had been summoned to London from their several homes, that they had met in the precincts of the court, and had drawn together as companions in misfortune. How far John Shakespeare afterwards conformed it is impossible to tell ; but in 1592 he is heard of as a recusant, his name appearing in a list of persons at Stratford who absented themselves from the parish church,—and moreover as one of those who had been mentioned in an earlier list of the same kind—which has not been preserved or discovered—those " heretofore presented." Among the Stratford recusants, in lists compiled on the spot, he was thus named on at least two occasions. In the list which has been preserved there is a note opposite the names of Mr. John Shakespeare, Mr. John Wheeler and several others, suggesting that their absence from church might be due to " fear of process for debt." But this remark seems to be no more than a good-natured attempt by some local authority to extenuate the matter. Nor is it easy to understand why the persons mentioned in the list should have avoided religious services for such a reason. Were they afraid of meeting process-servers if they ventured out of doors on Sunday ? And did they seclude themselves at home on the six other days of the week, never venturing to leave the threshold, or even to appear in their shops ?

When John Shakespeare was summoned before the Court of Queen's Bench in 1580, his eldest son had reached the age of sixteen. William Shakespeare was completing his course at the Grammar School of Stratford. The question of his future must have seriously occupied his father's mind. Clever boys from Stratford went up to Oxford. That both his father and his school-master were not ignorant of his capacity may be taken for granted ; but we cannot tell what projects for his son's future may have been considered by the elder Shakespeare, who was himself not destitute of energy and ambition ; nor what hopes the boy may then have entertained. No record ever found at Stratford does anything to illuminate this part of his life. No statement made by himself in later years has been preserved by any contemporary author. It is universally assumed that the profession of acting was not the one he at first adopted, and that he came to it after a short experience of some other calling in Stratford itself. On this subject tradition and report were busy long years after his own earthly career was over ; but these sources of information give no finality. What statements they offered, and what value they may have possessed, will be considered in another part of this work.

But Shakespeare was certainly still at Stratford in 1582,—the date of his marriage. A licence for its celebration was obtained in November of that year from the Bishop of Worcester ; his bride being Anne Hathaway, daughter of Richard Hathaway, a well-to-do farmer who resided at Shottery, a mile or two from the town. There was an old friendship between their fathers ; for many years before John Shakespeare had been surety for Richard Hathaway in a suit for debt. Little as we know about many poets, we know even less of their wives.   There is nothing that can be said about the wife of Edmund Spenser, Shakespeare's contemporary, whom he married in 1594.   Even her surname has never been certainly ascertained.[1]   Nor has much been learned about Anne Hathaway.   We cannot tell whether she was dark or fair, clever or commonplace.   Even her age is not so clearly established as might be wished.   Such details are usually ascertained from entries in a Parish Register, which records the Christening of children ; but Parish Registers are often defective, and no mention of Anne Hathaway's baptism has ever been found.   The date of her birth rests upon one piece of evidence alone.   On her grave in the chancel of Stratford Church is an inscription which states that she died in 1623 at the age of sixty-seven.   A simple calculation thus reveals that her birth took place in 1556 ; and Shakespeare was born eight years afterwards.   But the evidence is less decisive than it looks.   We have only the inscription on the tombstone, with its " 67 " in Arabic numerals ; and such figures are not always reliable, especially when the epitaph has been placed, like that of Mrs. Shakespeare, on the floor of the church, where it may be worn or defaced by the tread of many feet.   Errors easily arise.   It may be copied incorrectly by an antiquary, reading the figures in a dim light.   A workman may be employed to restore it, and may mistake a 7 for a 1, or a 1 for a 7, or a 3 for an 8. So long as no other evidence can be found, some doubt must always remain.

[1] This is no longer true of Spenser's wife.   A few fragments of information have been recovered.

The inscriptions on the Shakespeare tombs at Stratford were copied by, or for Dugdale and published in his *Antiquities of Warwickshire*, 1656. But Dugdale, or his informant has made at least one error in his numerals. He sets down in the epitaph of Mrs. Hall, Shakespeare's eldest daughter, the words—" She deceased the 2 day of July, Anno 1649." The Parish Register records the burial of Mrs. Hall on 16 July; and it is impossible that a fortnight elapsed between her death and burial. Dugdale's " 2 " cannot be right. But there are no means of correcting his mistake, for the inscription now to be seen in the church is only a modern restoration.

The circumstances of the marriage itself present another problem. The licence, as has been said, was granted by the Bishop of Worcester in November, 1582; and the ceremony must have followed at some church in the diocese which cannot now be identified. Susanna, the eldest child, was baptized at Stratford in May, 1583. But when these dates are used to suggest conclusions discreditable to the young husband and his wife, a wide field of discussion opens up. Questions arise concerning the marriage customs of England in the time of Elizabeth, which no layman can hope to settle for himself, and which even lawyers and antiquarians have not always illuminated.

In the sixteenth century the legal marriage and the religious ceremony had a distinct and separable existence; and the former might precede the latter by an appreciable space of time.

The words *pre-contract* and *troth-plight* have dropped out of the language; but they were familiar terms in the England of former days. A pre-contract was a ceremony performed in a private house, without the presence and authority of a priest, but before witnesses, by which a man and woman plighted their troth to each other : it resembled the Scotch irregular marriage, which is a fruitful source of litigation at the present day. No official record of it was made ; there was no documentary evidence of its existence ; but so long as the witnesses lived and were willing to testify to what they had seen and heard, the pre-contract was a binding engagement, and was accepted by the custom of the time as a perfect marriage. It might be, and often was, followed after a short interval of time by the ceremony in church ; but before the latter took place the pair lived as husband and wife without a hint of scandal. And in many cases the church wedding was dispensed with altogether.

Early writers on matrimony show clearly what was the familiar opinion. Henry Swinburne, a jurist, who was contemporary with Shakespeare, wrote a *Treatise of Sponsals or Matrimonial Contracts*, illustrated with copious citations from earlier authorities. In Swinburne's opinion the essence of marriage consists in the contract between a man and woman who take each other for husband and wife ; and all that is needed for complete matrimony is such a declaration in the presence of witnesses. Swinburne even raises the question whether a perfectly private acceptance, at which *no witnesses* are present, may constitute a valid marriage, and quotes authorities on both sides, inclining himself to the affirmative.

The subject is also discussed by Thomas Watson,

the last Catholic Bishop of Lincoln, in a sermon on marriage, contained in his book, *The Seven Sacraments of Christ's Church*. Although marriage is a sacrament, Bishop Watson considers that the presence of a priest is not necessary for its administration. The contract may be, and is commonly made by the parties themselves. The man takes the woman for his wife, and the woman takes him for her husband by a statement made in the presence of witnesses : nothing more is needed. Bishop Watson says :—

" Now when the two parties which marry together have done this and have said these words, then be they insured and justly married together, and be man and wife before God, and they cannot break this marriage in any wise after, as the man cannot marry another woman, nor the woman another man, so long as they be both alive. And if the two persons have sufficient record and witness to testify what they have done and said, then be they man and wife in the face of the world, and so before both God and man."

The ceremony in church is thus relegated by the Bishop to a secondary place. But, although it is not essential, it is desirable, none the less, that the actual marriage should be followed by the religious rite :—

" And notwithstanding that the man and woman consenting to be man and wife, and saying the words of the sacrament, be perfectly married together, yet the marriage of them in the face of the Church afterwards, by the ministration of the priest, is not superfluous, but most expedient for sundry causes."

Among the reasons adduced by the Bishop for the second marriage, the chief is that there may be a more certain

record, and that there may be no room for future doubt
or question.

Bishop Watson's view, reflecting as it does the common
usage and sentiment of his time, is so surprising to a
modern reader that his recent editor, Father Bridgett,
adds the comment :—

> " This sermon shows very clearly the reasons why the Council
> of Trent established the impediment of clandestinity. It
> seems to have been quite usual to contract marriage apart
> from the religious ceremony. The Bishop does not even
> seem to blame those who so acted, provided that they after-
> wards received the nuptial blessing, and renewed their contract
> before the Church."

A lawful marriage might thus exist between a man
and woman for weeks or months before they were
actually wedded at the altar, strange as it may appear
to modern eyes. A remarkable illustration of the fact
is pointed out by Halliwell-Phillipps, and occurs among
Shakespeare's own relations. His grandfather, Robert
Arden, had a daughter called Agnes. In a bond by
which part of his estate was settled upon his children,
Robert Arden speaks of her as " now the wife of Thomas
Stringer." The document is dated 17 July, 1550. But
if we inquire when the religious rites of marriage were
performed between Thomas Stringer and Agnes Arden
—her second marriage, for she had been a widow—the
answer may be found in the Register for the parish of
Bearley, which records their wedding on 15 October, 1550.
Just three months before the ceremony in church the
lady was living with Thomas Stringer as his wife, and

bearing his name, and they were recognized as a married pair by her father in a legal instrument.

If it now be asked, " But can we tell that William Shakespeare and Anne Hathaway were married by pre-contract or troth-plight, several months before the ecclesiastical ceremony, like other people of their time ? "— the natural answer is, " How can we tell that they were not ? " We cannot discuss their character and conduct on the basis of a negative assumption which is not supported by a shadow of evidence.

It is often suggested that the marriage was an unhappy one, and that the poet afterwards regretted the precipitation with which he entered into it. But Anne Hathaway may have been the most amiable and attractive of women. The epitaph placed upon her grave indicates that she had the affection of her children ; she had that of her husband when he married her, and there is no good reason to think that she lost it.

Three children were born of the marriage, Susanna in 1583, and twins, Hamnet and Judith, in 1585 ; and all were baptized at Stratford. But, although it may be believed that Shakespeare continued to reside there until at least his twenty-first year, there is no assured knowledge of the occupation he pursued ; nor do we know the date when he removed to London, and became an actor. Still less do we know what characteristics he displayed in opening manhood. On this subject his first biographers made very facile assumptions. They began with a notion that great poets, when young, are high-spirited, unconventional and undisciplined ; and applying it to Shakespeare, they told tales of his reckless and exuberant days at Stratford. There is no good evidence to support such tales ; and the generalization itself is nothing more than a romantic fancy. From what is recorded of Shakespeare's disposition, as it was revealed in later life, it is reasonable to think that his own lines would have afforded a more appropriate picture :—

> " The gravity and stillness of your youth
> The world hath noted, and your name is great
> In mouths of wisest censure."

Where our information about Shakespeare fails, it is reasonable to assume—unless good cause can be shown to the contrary—that he was very like other authors and shared their habits and tastes. Nothing but confusion and perplexity can come from a system which makes a gulf between the man and his works, only to be overcome by superhuman inspiration, and treats him alternately as a miracle of intellectual power and a prodigy of indifference to ordinary knowledge.

IV

THINGS WHICH NEVER WERE

When Michael Angelo was still alive, and all Italy was filled with his fame, several brief biographies of him were published. The most valuable was that of his friend and pupil, Ascanio Condivi, which opened with these words :—

"Some have written about this wonderful man who were not so intimate with him, I believe, as I have been. They have told, on one hand, things about him which never were, and on the other hand have omitted many things most worthy of being recorded."

Michael Angelo met with the common fate of all famous men. Events of significance in their lives have been left to forgetfulness, and the void is filled, in the words of Condivi, with *things which never were.*

Shakespeare has suffered with the rest, and more than many others. Even in his own lifetime, as in Michael Angelo's, the practice of relating *things which never were* had begun, and it continued intermittently through the seventeenth century and into the eighteenth.

It has been thought, and indeed not unnaturally, that Stratford would be rich in knowledge of the poet ; but all attempts made, within a hundred years after his time, to collect it were utterly disappointing, either from the insufficiency of the collectors, or from the actual lack of material.

The first who made notes about Shakespeare at Stratford was John Ward, Vicar of the parish in the time of Charles II. Ward had many opportunities, but used them in a manner so casual and uncritical as to make his testimony worthless. Nor has the poet gained in honour by his statements. The most celebrated among them is this :—

> " Shakespeare, Drayton, and Ben Jonson had a merry meeting, and, it seems, drank too hard, for Shakespeare died of a fever there contracted."

It will be observed that Ward himself offers the story with some hesitancy, and as little more than his own conjecture. Shakespeare drank too hard, and thus contracted a fever,—*it seems*. There is virtue in that *it seems*, as much as in many an *if*. Ward appears to have heard merely that Shakespeare received a friendly visit from Jonson and Drayton a short time before his death. He inferred that their presence had in some way hastened the poet's end. " How ? " inquired the musing vicar, and in a flash of inspiration he thought of undue festivity.

Ward published nothing. He kept a diary or commonplace-book in which he jotted down things which he had heard and his own comments upon them. It long remained in manuscript, and part of it is still un-

published ; but in 1839 extracts were given to the world
by Charles Severn, who took some pains to select the
more sensible portions. Even in the abbreviated form
there are such jottings as these : that the Egyptians kept
their wives at home by allowing them no shoes ; that
herring is a treacherous meat ; and that Woodstock men
are frequently long lived. Ward also states that Lambert, the Commonwealth general, and John Milton—his
own contemporaries—were Catholics in disguise and frequenters of Papist clubs ;—a piece of information which
has not found a place in their biographies. What the
unpublished part of the diary is like we can only conjecture.

On Ward's authority,—although even he hesitates a
little,—the statement that Shakespeare died of drink
has met in more works than one with a facile acceptance.
Medical authority does not support the notion. Death
may, indeed, be brought about by acute alcoholic poisoning, but not so readily as Ward imagines. In Shakespeare's time the more concentrated and dangerous forms
of alcohol were not in use ; and excessive drinking of ale
or wine could not produce fatal results. It is not even
established that intoxication caused by more fiery spirits
can do so. A doctor who has known in his own experience seventy cases of death from alcoholic poisoning
states that in all of them there were complicating causes,
of which exposure to cold was the most frequent. And
if it be suggested, to save the story, that Shakespeare
did not die from the immediate effects of drink, but
only as Ward actually states, of a fever induced by it,

the answer is that no such fever is known to medical science.

Nothing is stranger than the attempts which have been made—it is impossible to comprehend or imagine why—to justify Ward's supposition. He was, it is said, a University graduate ; but Universities have emitted from their portals many foolish persons with inaccurate minds. He could readily verify his tale by consulting Shakespeare's nephews, then living in Stratford ; but there is not a fragment of evidence to suggest that he did ; nor does it seem likely that he tried to verify his story of Milton as a frequenter of Papist clubs, or to throw a fuller light on the shoes of the wives of the Egyptians. The creator of Falstaff, it is added, must have been convivial in his disposition. It would be as reasonable to suggest that the creator of Macbeth could not have been averse to a little quiet assassination ; or that the creator of Captain Costigan must have been himself a tippler.

We do well to receive with peculiar caution stories concerning the deaths of famous men, even when the evidence in their favour may seem to be strong. When Pope Alexander VI died in the Vatican, after a very brief illness, rumours circulated in Rome which soon assumed definite shape and found a place in history. It was said that the Pope had fallen a victim to a murderous plot laid by himself and his son Cesare Borgia ; that they had conspired together to assassinate one of the Cardinals, whose wealth they coveted, by serving him at a banquet with poisoned wine, and that by the mistake of a servant the fatal cup was presented to the Pope's own lips. The story found universal credit. It was accepted by Guicciardini, who was himself a contemporary, and with whom as a searching inquirer it would be absurd to compare the Vicar of Stratford. Yet it was untrue and the Pope died of nothing more remarkable than an attack of malaria.

Some years after Ward made his transit across the stage, another inquirer appeared at Stratford. John Aubrey was a writer entitled to respect, and still has a modest place in literary history. The collection of brief biographies which he put together records a multitude of circumstances which would otherwise have been lost, and is of immense value when used with discrimination. Aubrey had a real sense of accuracy, and often took serious pains to verify his information ; but unfortunately that sense sometimes failed him utterly ; and things which are known, from other sources, to be untrue, and even impossible, find access to his pages. Aubrey never brought his biographical writings into any final shape, and never published them : at his death they were left in the saddest confusion—mere rough materials from which a book might have been constructed. He even sets down contradictory statements on the same subject, which he obtained at different times, and entered in different parts of his memoranda. Impartial posterity can but sift his evidence as best it may, by believing nothing merely because Aubrey reports it, and by tracing each several statement to the source from which it was derived. Sometimes his authority is good, and his evidence may be accepted,—as when he communicates information about Milton which he had received from the poet's widow and his brother : it is they who are the authorities, whilst Aubrey is only the intermediary. Sometimes, on his own admission, he is recording the idlest gossip.

Aubrey began his researches about Shakespeare in a hopeful manner. There was then in London an aged gentleman called William Beeston, whom Aubrey was advised by a friend to consult. Beeston had an interesting history. He was the son of Christopher Beeston who had been an actor in Elizabethan days, and a member of the same company with Shakespeare and Burbage. William Beeston himself had also been an actor and theatrical manager ; he was now living in retirement, but was visited by the younger men of letters, who listened to his tales of past times. Dryden himself took pleasure in his conversation, and was accustomed to call him " the Chronicle of the Stage."

What Aubrey heard from Beeston about the youth of Shakespeare is thus set down among his notes :—

" Though Ben Jonson says of him that he had but little Latin and less Greek, he understood Latin pretty well, for he had been in his younger days a schoolmaster in the country."

It is evident from the allusion to Latin that Beeston referred to a Grammar School in a country town ; and, as Shakespeare was resident when a young man in his native place, where his children were born in 1583 and 1585, the school could only be that of Stratford itself. Beeston was a man of intelligence and education ; he spoke in good faith, and transmitted an account of Shakespeare's early life which had been current long before in London amongst those who were his friends and daily associates. No tradition can ever be implicitly relied on ; but this is the best supported and most creditable of all.

However, Aubrey made another statement on another page of his jottings which has obtained a greater notoriety :—

" His father was a butcher, and I have been told heretofore by some of the neighbours that when he was a boy he exercised his father's trade ; but, when he killed a calf, he would do it in a high style and make a speech."

Aubrey has left us to choose between these statements, which plainly contradict each other, and admit of no reconciliation. The butcher story has an unmistakable flavour of the tap-room, and it is probable that Aubrey picked it up very casually from some one whom he found in a tavern behind a mug. We do not know the name of this individual ; but it is permissible to imagine that he belonged to the family of Sly. Unless the new Christopher Sly was exercising a primitive sense of humour at Aubrey's expense, and merely invented the story there and then—which is not impossible—we may conclude that it was current in Stratford about 1680 as one of the " old fond paradoxes, to make fools laugh i' the ale-house," of which Shakespeare speaks in *Othello*.

The story transmitted by Aubrey is more than improbable : it admits of positive disproof. Shakespeare's father is known from contemporary documents to have been a glover. Attempts have been made without much success to reconcile the two trades, and to argue that John Shakespeare may have been both a glover and a butcher ; but the occupations are quite incompatible. The making of gloves calls for a neatness and dexterity of touch which would be lost after much wielding of the pole-axe ; nor can we suppose that John Shakespeare killed an ox on Monday, stitched gloves on Tuesday, killed an ox on Wednesday, stitched gloves on Thursday, killed an ox on Friday, stitched gloves on Saturday, and rested on Sunday after the strain of his disparate exertions. It is as easy to believe that the same man could be both a tailor and a bricklayer.

Moreover, such a combination would have been contrary to the law and custom of the time. Tradesmen became after due apprenticeship members of their several companies ; and those who belonged to one craft were jealously debarred from encroaching upon the trade of others. And we cannot solve the story by arguing that, although Shakespeare's father was a glover, his son may have been apprenticed to a butcher, since the son does not always follow the occupation of the parent. We can only deal with the tale as we find it ; and Aubrey's informant reported that William Shakespeare was actually employed in his father's trade, and thus came to the killing of calves accompanied by poetical declamation. With the proof that the father was not a butcher the story vanishes into the air.

We have here stumbled upon one of the familiar processes of the tradition-maker. Like the narrator of fairy tales he has his familiar effects and his favourite strains of imagination. In his tales of famous men he starts from the notion that they began life as apprentice to some dull and mechanical occupation, but showed themselves lads of spirit, ran away from their master, and came at last to greatness. It is reported in Campbell's *Lives of the Admirals* that " young Cloudesley Shovell was put out apprentice to a mean trade, I think to that of a shoemaker." He then ran away to sea and became a cabin boy ; as Shakespeare in some accounts ran away to London and became a call-boy. In the real world and in sober truth, Sir Cloudesley Shovell belonged to a family of rank, and joined the Navy as the son of any such family might do. But if there were Baconians in naval as well as in literary history, it would be easy to argue that a shoemaker's apprentice could never have commanded a fleet ; and that something is seriously wrong, not in the unauthenticated story of his youth, which Baconians of course would accept, but in the belief that Cloudesley Shovell was ever an Admiral at all.

Another stage in the process of tradition-making followed. Having decided that Shakespeare was apprenticed to a trade and ran away from his master, the gossips then added the cause and occasion of his flight. Like other high-spirited youths Shakespeare was a poacher. He broke into the park of Sir Thomas Lucy at Charlecote and stole his deer ; Lucy prosecuted him, and he fled

to London.   But for this fortunate misfortune he would
have spent all his life at Stratford in a round of mechanical
toil, and the great world would never have heard of
him.

The time when this story arose can be shown with a
fair degree of precision,—it belongs to the last twenty
years of the seventeenth century.   When Aubrey visited
Stratford about 1680 it was still unknown.   John Aubrey
was a man of lively mind and infinite curiosity, a worthy
contemporary of Samuel Pepys.   He had an instinct for
telling and collecting stories, and loved them for their
fantastic or entertaining character.   Had he ever heard
of the poaching at Charlecote, he would not have failed
to note it.   Ward is equally silent, although he lived in
Stratford for many years, collected such things as he
heard, and was not restrained by a too distrustful mind.
The story which is now familiar to every tourist who
visits the place was quite unknown in the Stratford of
Charles II.

But we have now to make the acquaintance of another
story-teller.   Richard Davies was a country clergyman
who, after a very uneventful life, became Archdeacon of
Lichfield, and at his death left some curious memoranda which found a place in the Library of Corpus
Christi College, Oxford.   They contain the following
remarks about Shakespeare which have often been trans-
cribed :—

" Much given to all unluckinesse in stealing venison and
rabbits, particularly from Sir Lucy, who had him oft whipt,
and sometimes imprisoned, and at last made him fly his native

country, to his great advancement ; but his revenge was so great that he is his Justice Clodpate, and calls him a great man, and that, in allusion to his name, bore three lowses rampant for his arms."

Now nothing is known of Archdeacon Davies, who may have been very foolish or very wise ; and we can but seek some measure of his reliability in the document itself. He does not know the Christian name of Sir Thomas Lucy, whom he sets down merely as Sir Lucy ; although the information could have been obtained without laborious investigation. He also speaks of a " Justice Clodpate." Every reader of Shakespeare knows that there is no such character in his works ; but there is a Justice Clodpate, a foolish and conceited squire, in *Epsom-Wells* by Shadwell, which was first produced about 1672. Davies has confused him with Justice Shallow. These are small matters but not unimportant. It is not now in our power to question Archdeacon Davies, and to ask where he obtained his information, and on what grounds he accepted it. We can but test his story where testing is possible. Davies could have verified the name of the Justice by rising from his chair and taking down his Shakespeare from the shelf, or borrowing a Shakespeare, if he did not possess one. He did not trouble to do so. Can we believe that he took trouble about anything else, or entertained any notions of critical accuracy ?

This is the most famous of all the legends. It is familiar to multitudes who know little of Shakespeare's poetry ; just as in the popular notion of George Washington the incident of the hatchet, the cherry tree and the little prig dwarf the achievements of the soldier and statesman ; the one story having no more foundation than the other ; for the cherry tree has long since been given up by American historians. The poaching anecdote was published in 1709 by Nicholas Rowe, who derived it from the same source as the Archdeacon, whatever that may have been. We are usually referred on these occasions to some totally unknown individual somewhere behind the scenes.

The evidence of Davies and Rowe proves that the poaching story existed as a story about the year 1700 ; it proves that much and absolutely nothing more. Between 1585 or 1586, the supposed date of the incident, and 1700 there is a soundless gulf which no investigator has even attempted to bridge. A tale thus picked up casually, after the lapse of more than a hundred years, with no authority to support it but rumour, is perfectly worthless.

We are now divided by a similar tract of time from the early days of Wordsworth and Scott, Wellington and Nelson, and have the same means of knowing by tradition the events of their youth as Davies and Rowe had of knowing why Shakespeare left Stratford for London. Any of us may, if we please, communicate to the public a newly discovered incident in the boyhood or early manhood of Wordsworth or Scott, Wellington or Nelson, but if we could offer no evidence for it but a vague reference to common report, if our anecdote of Scott were something we had been told by somebody in Edinburgh or if our anecdote of Nelson were something we had been told by somebody in Portsmouth, no biographer would take it seriously.

The tradition of to-day is the gossip of yesterday ; and even in the occurrences of the moment report may be, as Petruchio calls it, a very liar. In the autumn of 1914, when the Great War had just begun, England was filled with rumours of Russian troops passing through on their way to France. They had been conveyed by sea from Archangel to the north of Scotland ; they were visible in trains, at railway junctions, at harbours and on steamers. There was endless talk of Russian faces and uniforms, and of friends and relatives who had actually seen them. The illustration is illuminating. If Shakespeare's deer-stalking be brought into comparison with the Russian soldiers, the advantage is all on the side of the latter. Their transit through England was a contemporary event, happening at that very hour ; it was not sunk by more than a hundred years in the depths of the past, and the number of witnesses who testified to it could be reckoned by thousands, all confident and assured.

Nor does the poaching story gain in plausibility by more minute investigation. The deer which the young Shakespeare is said to have stolen were not wild creatures roaming in the woods. The park at Charlecote, where imagination pictures him lurking at night with a crossbow, surrounds the mansion-house, and deer still graze beside it on the banks of the Avon. A stout oak fence, some miles in circuit, screens them from the highway, and prevents them from straying. Such parks were a luxury which English squires much cultivated, and their use was protected and restrained by law. From time immemorial the keeping of deer had been looked on as a royal prerogative, and jealously guarded. Subjects might be admitted to share it only with the consent of the Crown ; and a royal licence was essential before a deer park could be constructed and maintained.

The park at Charlecote, as we see it to-day, has certainly existed since the time of James I. But was there a park there during the reign of Elizabeth, and had Sir Thomas Lucy a licence to keep one ? On the answer to these questions much depends.

That there was no such park at a still earlier period, when Charlecote belonged to Lucy's father, is established by the evidence of John Leland, who travelled through the country and made careful notes of what he saw. Leland was interested in parks and recorded them with exactness. Near Warwick he passed three, whose names he mentions ; on his way to Stratford he saw another at Fulbrook ; but when he comes to Charlecote, he merely writes : " Here hath Mr. Lucy an ancient manor house on the left ripe of Avon."

There was no park then, it appears, at the date of Leland's visit. Had Sir Thomas Lucy, when he succeeded to the estate, and built the new and costly mansion, designed to form one, there was a procedure to be followed with which he must have been familiar : it was necessary, as has been said, to obtain a licence from the Crown. William Harrison, writing in 1577, makes the following statement :—

"It is trespass and against the law for any man to have or make a chase, park or free warren without good warranty of the King by his charter, or perfect title of prescription."

Harrison is confirmed by the words of the statute itself. In the fifth year of Elizabeth an Act was passed for the protection of game. It prescribes penalties for those who enter into any enclosed park, used for the keeping of deer, and wrongfully kill them ; but it contains also this very important qualification :—

"Provided always that this act, or anything therein contained, extend not to any park or enclosed ground hereafter to be made and used for deer, without the grant or licence of our sovereign lady the Queen, her heirs, successors or progenitors."

That Lucy must have been well acquainted with the statute every one will admit. Did he then take out a licence to enclose a park for deer on his estate ? Malone tells us that he searched the whole of the Patent Rolls for the reign of Elizabeth without finding the trace of such a grant. But, had he pursued the search a little further, he would have found a piece of material evidence. Sir Thomas Lucy died in 1600. He was succeeded by his son, a second Sir Thomas, who held the estates for only a few years, when they passed at his death to the grandson, Sir Thomas Lucy the third. It was this gentleman who actually took out a licence from the Crown to maintain a deer park at Charlecote. The document may

be seen in the Patent Rolls for James I. Its date is
1618. Sir Thomas Lucy the third is granted the right
to preserve and take game on his estates, and Charlecote
Park is expressly mentioned. Such licences were not
subject to renewal, in the modern manner, at stated
intervals, but were given, for good and all, to the gentlemen receiving them, their heirs and successors. The
fact that the grandson found it necessary to take out a
licence in 1618 suggests that the grandfather did not
possess one, and was not greatly interested in game
preserving.[1]

The legend contains other improbabilities. According
to an ancient and sound principle, a Justice of the Peace
cannot administer the law in cases where he himself is
concerned ; but Sir Thomas Lucy is both judge and
prosecutor in the matter of the Charlecote stag. He
then stretches his authority by inflicting an unauthorized
punishment. Davies relates that he pursued the young
Shakespeare with implacability, and *had him oft whipt*.
The statute of Elizabeth says nothing about whipping.
Poachers may be sentenced to three months imprison-
ment ; they must pay damages and find security to be of
good behaviour for seven years : that is all. If Sir
Thomas Lucy whipped Shakespeare, he went beyond
the Act of Parliament, and took the law into his own

[1] A document has been cited which mentions the gift of
a buck by the second Sir Thomas Lucy to Lord Keeper Eger-
ton in 1602. But it is one of the papers said to have been discovered at Bridgewater House by John Payne Collier,—in
other words, a forgery. It has deceived even the very elect.

hands. We can keep the Archdeacon's story on its feet only by supposing that Lucy had a park of doubtful legality, and practised an irregular and illegal form of chastisement.

It is not easy to estimate how far a landowner might then have acted with barefaced power and bade his will avouch it, when dealing with a homeless vagabond or even with a villager on his own estate. But Shakespeare did not come within either category : he belonged to a respectable family with an established place in the world ; and he did not live on Lucy's land. The remedy against poachers would have been to prosecute before the Justices in Session or to present a bill against them in the Star Chamber ; and Shakespeare, had he been subjected to personal violence, could have appealed to the Star Chamber for redress. But all that is known of Lucy suggests that he was a man of order and decorum, a pillar of the State, attached to all constitutional and established procedure,—not a man likely to be concerned in violent and unlawful actions.

The tale has been buttressed by the passage in *The Merry Wives of Windsor*, where Justice Shallow accuses Sir John Falstaff of stealing his deer, and an allusion is made to Shallow's coat-of-arms. By identifying the coat with that of Sir Thomas Lucy, it is believed that Shallow is himself identified with that gentleman ; and Shakespeare is then identified with the poacher : an ingenious but complicated deduction. But in truth Shallow bears no resemblance to Lucy ; their characters are opposed at every point. When Shallow first appears in *Henry IV*, he has not been in London for forty years or more ; London to him is a distant memory associated only with the foolish escapades of his youth ; he has spent the greater part of his life in his little property, with no associates but his own serving-men, and has grown very much to resemble them. Sir Thomas Lucy did not lead this hole-and-corner existence. He was a grave and dignified statesman, constantly in London and at Court, in favour with Elizabeth, and in the confidence of her ministers. He was commanded in 1583 to arrest Edward Arden of Park Hall on charges of treason, and to bring that important State prisoner in custody to London. He served as Sheriff of Warwickshire and sat in Parliament as member for the County. On one occasion he appears on a financial committee of the House, appointed to consider what subsidies should be granted to the Queen, along with Sir Philip Sidney and Sir Walter Raleigh. We cannot picture Justice Shallow on a Parliamentary committee, ejaculating in his foolish way, with Sir Philip Sidney on one side of him and Sir Walter Raleigh on the other.

Differing from Shallow in ability, character and manner of life, he differs from him in nothing so much as in religion and morals. Shallow has led an idle and dissolute existence in town during his youth, and in age dwells upon those happy and far-off days with cheery and boastful relish. He is a simple-minded old pagan. Lucy was a Puritan, zealous to further complete reformation by purging the Common Prayer Book and freeing it from superstitious ceremonies. He presented a petition to the House " touching the liberty of godly preachers," and for their settlement in parishes void of the means of salvation. We cannot conceive of Shallow engaged in such serious matters. Had it been suggested that Shakespeare revenged himself on Lucy by bringing him on the stage as Malvolio, the identification might have had some faint show of plausibility. Shallow is frankly impossible.

But a disparity of an even stranger kind may be noted. Shallow is not only unlike the real Lucy ; he is also unlike the Lucy of the legend itself. Sir Thomas is represented by Archdeacon Davies as a vindictive persecutor, who had Shakespeare whipped many times, and pursued him with such implacability that he compelled him at last to flee from his father and mother, his wife and children, and to take refuge in the distant capital. But Shallow is a good-natured creature incapable of bearing malice against a human being, and even of sustained resentment when he has suffered actual wrong. In *The Merry Wives of Windsor* he enters breathing out threats of vengeance against Falstaff, who has broken into his park and killed his deer, and vowing that if he were young again the sword should end it. Master Page, who loves peace and quietness, invites both the disputants to dine with him on a venison pasty and to drink down all unkindness. Shallow is instantly appeased ; the grievance vanishes into space ; Shallow and Falstaff are seated side by side at Page's friendly table, passing the sack, and all is forgotten and forgiven. Strange that Shakespeare should have revenged himself on a persistent and malignant enemy by representing him as the most pliant and placable of men !

The allusion to the coat-of-arms in *The Merry Wives of Windsor* calls for more minute inspection. Shallow there appears with his foolish cousin Slender and Sir Hugh Evans, the blundering Welshman. Slender celebrates the greatness of his kinsman ; he may write himself down as *Armigero*.

SHALLOW.   Ay, that I do ; and have done any time these three hundred years.

SLENDER.   All his successors gone before him hath done't ; and all his ancestors that come after him may : they may give the dozen white luces in their coat.

SHALLOW.   It is an old coat.

EVANS.   The dozen white louses do become an old coat well ; it agrees well, passant ; it is a familiar beast to man, and signifies love.

SHALLOW.   The luce is the fresh fish ; the salt-fish [1] is an old coat.

The luce spoken of is the pike, a now despised fish which was once esteemed as an article of food. Chaucer's Franklin, who loved good eating, had fat partridges in his mews and " many a luce " in his pond. Sir Thomas Lucy certainly bore as his arms three luces *hauriant*, i.e. rising to the surface. The pike is on his shield ; and the pike is said by Slender to be on Shallow's ; and without further ado Shallow and Lucy are thus made one.

But a closer study of this fragment of dialogue does

[1] It is " salt-fish " in the folio—with a hyphen.

not confirm the argument. It was not the Charlecote family alone that bore the luces ; and it is not even certain, after all, that they are understood to be the genuine arms of Justice Shallow. Slender does, indeed, attribute to him " the dozen white luces " ; but Slender lives in a state of mental confusion ; he has just spoken of successors that have gone before and ancestors that come after ; and Shakespeare would not assign to such a muddler a correct recital of heraldic blazonings. After his allusion to the luces, Shallow remarks, " It is an *old* coat,"—apparently, from what comes after, to correct him and make a protest. Sir Hugh Evans interposes with his absurd observation about the louse, the familiar beast to man. Shallow, who has paid no attention to him, and has continued the train of his own reflections, then adds, " The luce is the fresh fish : the salt-fish is an old coat," i.e. the old coat of which he has just spoken, his own. The meaning seems to be that Slender is in error ; and that the arms of which Shallow speaks are not the luces, but a salt-fish which he thinks more appropriate to long descent. This remark appears to turn upon the antithesis of *fresh* and *old*. Being only a fresh fish, the luce might be suitable to a new family, which had no ancestral honours ; but a family so very old as Shallow's must needs have a salt-fish, which is ancient indeed. Shakespeare knew that a remark about the antiquity of salt-fish would send a smile round the theatre. Familiarly known as " poor-John " it was a common but unwelcome article of diet, and the theme of rueful jests. " Very ancient and fish-like " says

Stephano in *The Tempest*. Shallow's repudiation of the luces, and his preference for a salt-fish as his heraldic emblem, take us far away from Charlecote and its squire.

And Shakespeare had no need to go there in order to find a hint for Slender's talk about luces on a coat. He could easily find one in London. The Company of Fishmongers bore a shield on which three dolphins were emblazoned between two pairs of luces ; and to Shakespeare's audience the mention of such bearings would naturally suggest the Company of Fishmongers, rather than the Warwickshire squire. Pageants and processions, in which the Companies passed through the streets, with much display of their arms on banners and triumphal cars, were familiar events ; and the luces of the Fishmongers were often to the seen.

Shakespeare began to write *The Merry Wives of Windsor* with no intention but to create an amusing scene. He introduced the foolish justice and his friends, uttering nonsense and making absurd pretensions to gentility. Talk about local importance and a long pedigree naturally led to a coat-of-arms. Any coat would do, provided it could be made an occasion of jest. Shakespeare thought of luces, which may have occurred to him from a recent glance at the arms of the Fishmongers ; and he thus introduced the jokes about louses and " a kind of not of the newest poor-John." That his audience suspected anything more is improbable, and that they connected the scene with Sir Thomas Lucy is more improbable still. The similarity of the arms to those of the Charlecote family is a coincidence and nothing more. Such coincidences are the peculiar bane of historical research. They lie in wait at every turn, but only the experienced investigator is on his guard against them.

There is, upon this interpretation, no visible ground for identifying Shallow with Lucy. And there are further objections of another kind. The belief that Shakespeare retaliated in *The Merry Wives of Windsor* for a grievance of such ancient date is in itself hard to accept. The play was first published in 1602, and it cannot have been written earlier than 1598 or 1599. Shakespeare was then at the height of his prosperity and fame. The date which is commonly assigned to the poaching affair is 1585 or 1586 ; in any computation the interval of time between Shakespeare's departure from Stratford and the composition of *The Merry Wives of Windsor* cannot have been less than ten years and may have been fifteen. For ten or fifteen years, we are to understand, Shakespeare nursed his wrath to keep it warm, before taking the great revenge attributed to him by the Lichfield divine. They were years of immense and varied activity, new interests arising, new friends gathering round him, the absorbing ardour of literary composition. It is one of the commonest experiences of life that in the space of time between youth and middle-age many things sink into oblivion. Each of us, like Petrarch, looks back upon a past where he himself is almost a stranger—" Questo era in parte altr' uom da quel ch'i' sono." Other themes and associations fill our thoughts, and old memories fade away. That Shakespeare after so many years of social life and imaginative toil in London should still have dwelt in this manner on his youth at Stratford is hard to believe. It is not in human nature.

As the eighteenth century advanced, a more discriminating spirit appeared, and Shakespeare's biography was dealt with in a scholarly manner; but deliberate invention came also into play, aided sometimes by forgery. It is not clear how far the story now to be told was actually manufactured. After its first publication in 1753 it was taken up by Dr. Johnson, who set it forth in the dignity of his own prose. When Shakespeare, it is said, came to London poor and friendless, he stood at the door of the theatre, and held the horses of the playgoers. While thus engaged he became so conspicuous for his care and readiness that every one called for Will Shakespeare, and scarce any other waiter was trusted with a horse when Shakespeare was to be had. Holding horses is notoriously an office almost as delicate as that of Nanky Poo when he passed round the hat, and calls for a rare combination of dexterity and trustworthiness. Finding more horses put into his hands than he could deal with, he hired boys to hold them under his supervision, who, when Will Shakespeare was summoned, were immediately to present themselves,—" I am Shakespeare's boy, Sir." Thus far Dr. Johnson. His sturdy incredulity was for once laid singularly to sleep.

We have but to ask how the knowledge of these occurrences was transmitted, without documents of any sort from about 1587 to 1753, through so many generations of mortal men. It is said that Sir William Davenant told the tale to Betterton, who told it to Rowe, who told it to Pope, who told it to Bishop Newton, who told it to some one else, who told it to the actual writer. We are reminded of Sir Benjamin Backbite authenticating his story of the imaginary duel between Sir Peter Teazle and his nephew,—" I tell you I had it from one, who had it from one, who had it from one." The genealogy is as weak as all such genealogies must be, and is made even weaker by the fact that Nicholas Rowe, who figures as one of the links in the chain, does not mention the anecdote in the life of Shakespeare which he actually wrote.

Tradition is occupied with Shakespeare's early youth, and advances by stages, presenting first his apprentice-ship as a boy, then his flight from Stratford, then his first adventurous occupation in town. We seem to be looking on during the gradual formation of a fairy tale, in which Shakespeare is assuming a marked resemblance to Dick Whittington—the Whittington of legend, not the authentic Lord Mayor of London. But had tradition possessed authentic value, we should rather have found reminiscences of his later days, when his celebrity was established, when curiosity about him was most keen, and information would be eagerly acquired and passed on. But concerning these supreme years of fame and honour, when his name was familiar to every educated man in England, the late traditions are utterly silent; whilst they fill up the tale of his boyhood and youth, when his affairs interested none but himself and his small private circle, and were least likely to be remembered. The persons who transmitted them, when they can be traced, are bad witnesses, displaying the most easy credulity and indifference to all authentication, hopelessly wrong when they venture upon details that can be verified. But there are still biographers, not of Shakespeare alone, who quote the statement of some very obscure and obviously muddled individual in the seventeenth century with as much confidence as if it had been transmitted after searching inquiry by Sir Isaac Newton.

The notion that Shakespeare arrived in London in poverty, and without a friend, and led for some years a Bohemian existence, is familiar to all; but it rests upon no real authority. We know of no reason why he should leave Stratford except the promptings of ambition; and it is natural to suppose that he chose his own time, and went to London when he could do so with most convenience. We hear nothing of any estrangement from his own family, and John Shakespeare was not so reduced in the world that he could do nothing for his eldest son.

At the very time when Shakespeare is supposed to have been holding horses in the streets for a livelihood, his parents made another attempt to recover the farm at Asbies, which had been mortgaged. Edmund Lambert, who held the property, died in April, 1587; his claim descended to his son; John and Mary Shakespeare then approached the younger Lambert, tendered the sum of £40, the amount for which the land had been pledged, and asked that the mortgage should be cancelled and the property restored to them. The negotiations were unsuccessful ; the farm was not recovered ; but the Shakespeares were left at least with the £40 in hand. Their affairs cannot have been hopelessly embarrassed when they were able to contemplate such a transaction involving so large a sum. And if John and Mary Shakespeare, having £40 at their disposal, actually believed that to recover the farm of Asbies was of more importance than to save their son from destitution, they must have been very unnatural parents. Nor have biographers paused to inquire what meanwhile had become of Shakespeare's wife and his three children. Were they living at Stratford on charity ? Or did Shakespeare find horse-holding so profitable as to be able to send them remittances from London ?

It is strange also that the rude occupations and Bohemian beginnings should be mentioned by none of Shakespeare's contemporaries. The Elizabethans were not wont to draw a veil over anything that might serve as a subject of raillery against each other. Ben Jonson, when he left school, was apprenticed to a bricklayer ; and he was never allowed to forget the fact as long as he lived. Allusions to Ben's bricks and mortar flowed easily and copiously from the pens of his brother poets. Gabriel Harvey was the son of a rope-maker, and was freely taunted with ropes. But of Shakespeare's menial origin there is not a word. Robert Greene, whose fame as a dramatist was sadly eclipsed by his rise, regarded him with malignant envy, and wrote a violent attack on the new-comer. Yet Greene has nothing to say except

that Shakespeare is a mere actor, who has trod the
boards in the plays of better men, and is now presum-
ing to rival them by writing plays himself. Of killing
calves, stealing deer, and holding horses, there is not a
word; although if Greene had ever heard of such
things he would have poured them forth with eager
volubility.

Soon after Shakespeare had received his coat-of-arms,
a scandalous quarrel took place in the Heralds' Office.
Ralph Brooke, the York Herald, a man of jealous and
surly temper, plunged into a feud with his colleagues,
and to discredit them attacked the grants of coat-armour
which they had recently made. He composed a long
and savage document. Numerous persons to whom
arms had been given were named by Brooke, and their
unworthiness exposed. They were men of mean estate
and mechanical occupation; one was the son of a pedlar,
another a maker of stockings, another a haberdasher,
another a printer,—all base fellows indeed, favoured by
officials unworthy of their place.

The story of Shakespeare's youth might well have
afforded Ralph Brooke an occasion for anti-Stratfordian
eloquence. We may imgaine the triumph of the recalci-
trant Herald,—" This John Shakespeare who had received
arms is a bankrupt tradesman. His son William, the
real mover in the affair, was apprenticed to a butcher,
became a poacher, ran away from his indigent home,
and earned a few coppers by holding horses at a theatre
door." But Brooke had no information of such a kind.
He actually did make a protest against the Shakespeare

arms ; but advanced only the mild objection that they bore too close a resemblance to those which already belonged to another family,—a technical point and nothing more. It was the only objection which his malign spirit and active inquiry could discover.

Robert Greene is silent, Ralph Brooke is silent, when both Greene and Brooke were ready to present Shakespeare's life and character in a degrading light, if they could possibly do so. Neither Greene nor Brooke had ever heard the now familiar tale.

Another story figures in the Apocrypha, which cannot be traced to an earlier date than 1762, when it was related to a curious traveller in the village inn at Bidford. It sadly illustrates the fate of a great name when it falls among the *bassa gente*. Once on a time an English traveller having heard in Rome much talk about Cicero from the guide who escorted him over the Forum, asked who Cicero may have been, and was answered with perfect confidence, "An enormous giant." The frequenters of the Bidford inn, who knew Shakespeare only by name as a famous man of former days, thought of him as an enormous toper ; and related that he once came from Stratford with a company of revellers, drank deep at Bidford, became helplessly intoxicated, and spent the night in a drunken sleep under a crab-tree.

This story, it has been said, is first heard of in 1762. Just three years afterwards a little book was printed in Scotland which is entitled *The Witty and Entertaining Exploits of George Buchanan*. Its hero is the famous humanist, who wrote with classical Latinity, was a poet

and historian, and acted as tutor to James I. Long
after his death he was transformed by popular report
into another George Buchanan, who served the king as
his Jester, and played many merry pranks, few of them
fit for recital in polite society, yet somehow continued
to be a man of intellect and a scholar. The second
George Buchanan displaced the first in the popular
mind, and to this day there are persons in Scotland who
are familiar with the disreputable drolleries of George
Buchanan the King's Fool, but have never heard of the
humanist, and refuse to believe in his existence.

Halliwell-Phillipps, whose unaccountable liking for
" traditional stories " and " rural versions " has immensely impaired the value of his researches, and even
done serious injury to Shakespeare's name, actually
accepted the tale of the drinking bout and the Bidford
crab-tree. Whether he also believed stories told of
Buchanan to be authentic history, it is impossible to
tell.

The theories of Halliwell-Phillipps are inconsistent
enough. He was a firm believer in the illiteracy of
Stratford, he was even the most conspicuous exponent
of the doctrine ; but he was also convinced that for a
hundred years after Shakespeare's time the chief events
in his life were familiar to every one in the place, having
been handed down from father to son by oral tradition.
People do not talk of something which does not interest
them ; those who cannot read are not interested in books,
and are still less likely to concern themselves about the
unknown individuals by whom the books were written.

If the inhabitants of Stratford had been as ignorant as
Halliwell-Phillipps imagined, they would have known as
much about Shakespeare a hundred years after his death
as they did about the builders of Stonehenge.

Even in a society which cannot be dismissed as illiterate
the attention given to an author's personal history may
be neither widespread nor persistent ; and more modern
examples have shown how little is known of it in his own
native district. The people of Lincolnshire in Tenny-
son's lifetime had almost forgotten him ; and Canon
Rawnsley, who spent his youth in the very part of the
country where he was born and brought up, tells us that
even then little real interest was taken in him or his
fame, and that his works were seldom to be met with in
the houses of rich or poor in the very neighbourhood.

At a later time he endeavoured to collect information
concerning Wordsworth among the peasants of Grasmere,
with somewhat slender results.[1]

Yet the conditions were peculiarly favourable. Canon
Rawnsley was not seeking to collect traditions, transmitted
from father to son, about a poet who had lived a century
before. Only twenty years had passed since Wordsworth's death, and many individuals could be found
who had personally known him. But there was no
corresponding knowledge of his poetry, which seemed
to be quite unread among the dalesmen ; and a notion
prevailed that the best part of it had been written by

[1] " Reminiscences of Wordsworth amongst the Peasantry
of Westmorland," H. D. Rawnsley, *Wordsworthiana*, 1889,
p. 79.

Hartley Coleridge. There was " a sort of disbelief among the natives in the poet's greatness " ; and ludicrous tales were told of his walks on the roads around Grasmere, where he went mumbling and muttering by himself, and children were scared in the twilight by the booming of his voice.

It is still reported that some of the peasants could explain this habit only as a sign of insanity ; and that when a native of the valley once returned to his home, and asked for the news of the countryside, he was told that there was no great news, but old Wordsworth had broken out again.

With the authentic knowledge of Wordsworth's life which we possess, it is sobering to consider what his biography might have been, if its compilers had resorted to such sources as these for their information, and had left for the bewilderment of future generations, the strange picture of a mumbling but crafty lunatic, publishing as his own the works of Hartley Coleridge. Tracing the hand of Hartley Coleridge in the poems attributed to Wordsworth might have become a popular pastime, like digging in Shakespeare's earlier plays for strata of Marlowe and Greene.

V

THE STRANGE CONSPIRACY

The works of Shakespeare were not published anonymously in his own day, and attributed to him three hundred years afterwards by the hazardous conjectures of modern scholars ; although the arguments used by Baconians would seem to suggest as much. In 1623 when the complete collection appeared in the Folio, it was entitled *Mr. William Shakespeare's Comedies, Histories and Tragedies*. His portrait was placed in the volume ; and the dramas were declared to be Shakespeare's by four very sound and reliable witnesses—John Heming, Henry Condell, Ben Jonson, and Leonard Digges.

Heming and Condell were members of the theatrical company which produced the plays, and with which Shakespeare himself was associated ; they had belonged to it for many years, and were familiar with all its affairs. They knew who wrote the comedies, histories and tragedies ; they could not help but know : and they ascribed them, as the most obvious thing in the world, to Shakespeare, never dreaming of doubt or difficulty. " We have but collected them," they wrote, " and done

an office to the dead, to procure his orphans guardians ;
without ambition of self-profit or fame, only to keep
the memory of so worthy a friend and fellow alive as
was our Shakespeare." It is natural to believe, unless
weighty reasons can be adduced to the contrary, that
these words were simply and sincerely written, and told
nothing more than the plain truth. And they added,
" We have scarce received from him a blot in his papers."
Heming and Condell, who had long been the business
managers of the company, could not have said in plainer
terms that they had received the manuscripts of the
plays from Shakespeare and that he had been author of
them.

Ben Jonson was then the greatest poet and dramatist
in England ; his plays had been produced by the same
company as Shakespeare's ; and Shakespeare had
appeared in them on the stage. Jonson had known
him for many years, and respected and admired him :
we have his own authority for saying so. " I loved the
man," he wrote, " and do honour his memory on this
side idolatry as much as any." He contributed to the
Folio the long poem which has been already quoted,
and entitled it :—

" *To the Memory of my beloved the Author, Mr. William
Shakespeare, and what he hath left us.*"

And he leaves us in no doubt as to the personality and
birthplace of the poet whom he celebrates.

> " Look, how the father's face
> Lives in his issue ; even so the race

Of Shakespeare's mind and manners brightly shines
In his well-turned and true-filed lines ;
In each of which he seems to shake a lance
As brandished at the eyes of Ignorance.
Sweet Swan of Avon, what a sight it were
To see thee in our waters yet appear ;
And make those flights upon the banks of Thames
That so did take Eliza and our James."

Jonson thus indicates that the plays which were acted at Whitehall, Greenwich and Richmond before the Court, which delighted Elizabeth and James I, were written by the poet from Stratford. " Sweet Swan of Avon " has an obvious significance. And he is aware of no incompatibility between " Shakespeare's mind and manners " and the contents and tone of the works attributed to him. On the contrary, he states that " Shakespeare's mind and manners "—it is his own phrase —are expressed and reflected there ; that, having known Shakespeare in his lifetime, he recognizes his thoughts and feelings in the plays themselves.

Some verses were also contributed by Leonard Digges of University College, Oxford, a man of learning and an ardent admirer of the poet. They begin :—

" Shakespeare, at length thy pious fellows give
The world thy works ; thy works by which outline
Thy tomb thy name must : when that stone is rent,
And time dissolves thy Stratford monument,
Here we alive shall view thee still. This book
When brass and marble fade, shall make thee look
Fresh to all ages."

Not very wonderful as poetry, but valuable as evidence. Shakespeare's works are sure of poetic immortality; and they were written, Digges tells us, by one who was a member of the same dramatic company as Heming and Condell, his " pious fellows "—and whose tomb might be seen at Stratford-on-Avon.

Heming, Condell, Jonson and Digges are all contemporaries, all well acquainted with the facts, unanimous in their attestation of Shakespeare's authorship, and their quiet but significant assumption that there is no need of proof, that no one has ever disputed it. No better testimony to the authorship of any work written three centuries ago is anywhere to be found. If such evidence is to go for nothing, then all books are fatherless, unless we have written them ourselves, or seen them written with our own eyes.

On what grounds, if we reject this testimony for Shakespeare, can we attribute the *Æneid* to Virgil, or the *Epistle to the Romans* to St. Paul? There are no contemporary witnesses for either; no writer in the age of Augustus states that Virgil wrote the *Æneid*, no writer in the first century states that St. Paul wrote the Epistle: the case for both is immensely weaker than that for Shakespeare. Both, also, are very openly exposed to the familiar arguments by which Shakespeare is discredited. Virgil was a farmer's son; and a farmer's son is a being whom no good Baconian can contemplate without a shudder of horror and repulsion. St. Paul was a craftsman, a maker of tents, who worked with his own hands for a livelihood. How could he, on

Baconian principles, have possessed such subtlety of intellect as is manifested in the Epistle ? How could he have addressed the Athenians, an intelligent and critical audience, in the Areopagus, read Greek poets and quoted Menander ? Little will be left of Virgil and St. Paul when the Baconian artillery has been fairly trained upon them.

With such knowledge of Shakespeare's personality as we now possess, we cannot argue that Heming and Condell, Jonson and Digges must be wrong. They are themselves the source of our information, the very fountainhead. They are the touchstone by which the probability of all statements about Shakespeare made at a later date must be tested. It is manifest that Heming, Condell, Jonson and Digges did not think of him as a dull and illiterate man of rustic extraction : they thought of him as a delightful companion and a poet of the highest genius ; they said so in terms which cannot be misunderstood. We cannot set our opinion of Shakespeare against theirs ; for they were his friends and contemporaries, and no man now living in the world has ever seen his face or heard his voice.

It is useless to contend that Shakespeare's authorship is inconsistent with stories that were told long after his death and impressions about him which may be entertained at the present day. Contemporary evidence is the only thing that matters ; and if the stories and impressions fail to accord with it, so much the worse for the stories and impressions. Nor, with such evidence before us, need we ask for general considerations to

show that Shakespeare was qualified by capacity or
education for the authorship of the plays. The fact
that he wrote them is established by good witnesses,
and is sufficient proof that he was able to do so. Whatever theory we may form of Shakespeare as a man, it
must be consistent with his authorship of the comedies,
histories and tragedies,—unless Heming, Condell, Jonson
and Digges were bereft of their wits or contriving some
monstrous deception. That they were actually insane
no one will pretend ; and nothing remains for the
Baconian but the hypothesis of conspiracy. It is then
for him to explain what the conspiracy was, and why
these men so strangely entered into it.

This is what he must maintain, if his theory is ever
to be accepted as historical fact,—that, after Bacon had
written the plays, he formed a scheme to delude the
public by attributing them to William Shakespeare, a
member of the company which accepted and performed
them. Bacon could not have done this by his own
unaided efforts ; he had allies and fellow-conspirators,
who combined together to support him in his remarkable
project. Heming, Condell, Jonson and Digges were
among them. Bacon was still alive in 1623 when the
Folio was published, and must be supposed to have
taken some interest in its preparation. Under his
instructions these men acted a part and made false
professions. Heming and Condell subscribed to a
preface in which they spoke of their deceased friend
and colleague as the author. They were even so daring
as to write :—

" It had been a thing, we confess worthy to have been wished that the Author himself had lived to have set forth and over-seen his own writings. But since it hath been ordained other-wise, and he by death departed from that right, we pray you do not envy his Friends the office of their care and pain, to have collected and published them."

In presence of such audacious deception as the Baconians must believe this to have been, they may well be amazed. These incredible knaves knew that their friend and fellow-actor was incapable of writing the works which they had in their possession, and were seeing through the press; they knew that the real author was not dead at all; that he was alive and well and capable of editing and publishing the book himself. But Ben Jonson excelled Heming and Condell, if that be possible, in his soaring mendacity. He inserted his verses—*To the Memory of my beloved, the Author, Mr. William Shakespeare, and what he hath left us,*—knowing that Shakespeare was not the author, and that the real author was Francis Bacon, the former Lord Chancellor, now residing in his chambers at Gray's Inn, and cog-nizant of the whole transaction. Jonson was so resolved to mystify the public, at whatever expense to his own honesty, that he also placed in the Folio another piece of verse, which stands opposite Shakespeare's portrait :—

> " The Figure that thou here seest put,
> It was for gentle Shakespeare cut ;
> Wherein the Graver had a strife
> With Nature to outdo the life.

> O could he but have drawn his wit
> As well in brass, as he hath hit
> His face ! the Print would then surpass
> All that was ever writ in brass.
> But, since he cannot, Reader, look
> Not on his Picture, but his Book."

The insertion of a portrait of Shakespeare, as that of the author, in a work actually written by Bacon, was itself a startling device. Jonson lent his support to the trick ; and exhorted the public to look for the real likeness of Shakespeare in his Book,—which he knew to be Bacon's Book, not Shakespeare's !

It is incumbent on the Baconians to offer some reason for such mysterious behaviour. Were these men bribed by Bacon ? Or did they forswear themselves merely to please him ; were they humble and subservient instruments, self-effacing adherents and acolytes of the prophet at Gray's Inn ? It is not in Jonson's character, for he was a man of the strongest fibre, distinguished by his stout and surly independence. And there is no evidence to suggest that Heming and Condell had ever known or spoken to Bacon in all their lives. We cannot be setting forth in the open way to truth when such baffling difficulties arise to beset us.

But we are still only at the beginning of the complications which emerge. The association of Shakespeare's name with the plays was not a new thing when the Folio was published in 1623. Long before that date he had been mentioned by contemporary authors as the writer of the dramas ; and single plays had been published with his name on the title page. In 1593 *Venus and Adonis* was given to the world with a dedication signed *William Shakespeare*. In 1594 another poem, *The Rape of Lucrece*, came from the press with a dedication signed *William Shakespeare*. If Shakespeare was all that the Baconians tell us he was, he could no more have written these poems than the plays themselves. Bacon's was the hand that guided the pen ; the William Shakespeare who signed the dedication was Bacon, using a pseudonym. His selection of such a name was dangerous. It was not an invention, like " Stendhal " or " George Eliot," but that of a real and living man, who was then well known in London as a member of the company of actors led by Richard Burbage. Stratfordians find no difficulty. They believe that the William Shakespeare who signed the dedication to *The Rape of Lucrece* in 1594, and the William Shakespeare who acted with his company before Queen Elizabeth at the Christmas of 1594, were one and the same person. Baconians believe that the poem was written by Bacon, that he was unwilling to publish it under his own name, unwilling, for some reason which we cannot even imagine, to issue it anonymously, and selected as his pseudonym the name of the well-known actor. And under the same name he produced his brilliant series of plays.

He thus set up a pretender, whose claims were universally accepted, and compromised his right to his own work. We need not pause to comment on the foolishness of his conduct, it is astonishing in a man of so much shrewdness and foresight as Bacon.

A number of questions now spring up and call for consideration. What did the well-known actor himself think about it all ? Was he personally acquainted with Bacon, and did he consent to the use of his name by the latter as a disguise ? If he did Bacon this service, was it out of disinterested amicability, or because he had received some gratification from Bacon's easily-depleted purse ? Or did Bacon omit to consult him before taking liberties with something which certainly belonged to him,—his Christian name and surname ; did he learn of it first with amazement when he saw *Venus and Adonis* and *Lucrece* on the bookstalls ; was he amazed ; and did he air his grievance in taverns and other places of public resort ?

And what did Burbage and the members of his company think about it all? The situation was one which must have keenly excited their curiosity and interest. Dramas of the most wonderful kind were handed to them for representation ; these dramas were given out as the work of their colleague, William Shakespeare. They knew very well—on Baconian premises—that Shakespeare could not possibly be the author. He was in their society every day ; they met him at rehearsals and performances, and travelled with him on tour ; heard his stupid and empty talk ; knew that he had neither intelligence nor education. However Shakespeare may have imposed on modern scholarship, he could not possibly have imposed on his fellow-actors. The plays which they were performing, masterpieces of dramatic power and poetic eloquence, were given to the world as his, acted as his, published as his. Did they make no sort of protest, hint at no scandal ? If they observed a complete and tactful silence under these extraordinary circumstances, at least one thing may be taken for certain,—that the members of Burbage's company were more free from envy and jealousy than any other set of men that ever lived.

Those actors behaved like sportsmen. They saw one of their number singled out for a dazzling and quite unmerited distinction, honoured as the author of the marvellous plays which they presented at the Globe and the Blackfriars, and of which, as they well knew, he could not have written a line ; but their minds remained unruffled by spasms of annoyance. They kept the secret, which to them was a very open one. The identity of the real author was known at least to the leaders, who received the manuscripts from Bacon ; and it can hardly have been concealed from the rest. The plays themselves show a knowledge of dramatic technique, which could not have been acquired except by assiduous frequentation of the stage. There are indications of parts adapted for performance by certain actors, whose peculiarities of appearance and manner the author had before his mind as he wrote. Nor is it usual to put a play through rehearsal without at least the occasional presence of the author on the boards, to discuss certain scenes and effects with the producer. For all these reasons the writer of the plays must have frequently visited the Globe.

It has not been suggested that Bacon himself actually

performed in the theatre, under the name of William Shakespeare, although this is an extension of the theory which might simplify it ; but as a dramatic author his personality must have been familiar to the actors. Many times over they saw the immense felt hat and the heavy brown beard on the stage of the Globe at rehearsals. and heard the voice of Bacon as he conferred with Burbage, That Bacon refused to give his own name to the pieces, and actually bestowed the titular honours on a member of the company, not even its most distinguished member, could not but have caused lively discussion among them, But, although actors are not the most reticent of men. not a hint of the secret was allowed to escape. Burbage's company joined to promote the deception ; and its last survivors kept it in being long after Burbage and Shakespeare, and Heming and Condell, and Bacon himself were dead.

In the last days of that famous association, when Charles I was King, and all its founders were gone, the leadership devolved upon two seniors who remembered its golden times, John Lowin and Joseph Taylor. An enterprising publisher proposed to print the plays of Beaumont and Fletcher, which belonged to the company, received permission to do so, and issued them in a folio volume which appeared in 1647. It is dedicated by the actors to the Earl of Pembroke and Montgomery, the survivor of the two noble brethren to whom Heming and Condell had dedicated the Folio of 1623 ; they remind the Earl of that occasion and example, and ask him to give the same patronage to Beaumont and Fletcher which he and his elder brother had formerly given " to the flowing compositions of the then expired Sweet Swan of Avon, Shakespeare." The dedication is signed by, amongst others, John Lowin and Joseph Taylor.

To the Stratfordian, happy in the directness and simplicity of his views, this seems a most natural and innocent transaction. The Baconian must see it in a different light. He cannot suppose that Lowin and Taylor were under a delusion ; they knew that Shakespeare was an impostor ; every one connected with the company must have known it. They were in the secret, and were seeking to delude the public by continuing the mystification. But their conduct was perfectly motiveless. Bacon had been dead for more than twenty years ; justice to his memory would have suggested that now, even at this late hour, he should receive the honour due to his dramatic achievements ; and the divulgence of his authorship would have made no small sensation. Some reason should be suggested why, after the lapse of so many years, Lowin and Taylor should have kept up the old pretence, and continued to deceive their fellow-men.

Shakespeare, according to the Baconians, was an ignorant lout from the country, who had somehow pushed his way on to the stage. They do not even pause to consider the incoherence of the portrait they present. Shakespeare is a rustic fresh from agricultural toil, and he is also a member of a company of actors which was favoured by the Crown and gave representations at the

Palace. We are told by a contemporary that he played
" some kingly parts,"—that is, that he impersonated
royalty in certain dramas. In the performance of these
parts, in the presence of royalty itself, grace, dignity
and refinement of bearing, and speech are essential ; if
Bacon had assigned them to a raw and awkward countryman, he would have brought ridicule on his company,
and would have shown small respect for his art, his
audience or his prospects.

Regardless of such reflections, the Baconians make
Shakespeare a mere bucolic. His authorship is impossible. In most Baconian books there are expressions
of surprise and amusement at the folly of the Stratfordians who accept anything so absurd.   But if the theory
be true, and the idea that William Shakespeare wrote the
plays be indeed grotesque, then the folly of the Stratfordians is nothing to that which must be attributed to
Bacon himself. He wished to disguise his authorship,
and caused his work to be acted in the theatre, and
at Court in presence of Elizabeth and James, under the
name of the man of Stratford. Bacon might have
chosen a more plausible mask,—some scholar from
Oxford, who had failed of promotion and might be
tempted to lend his name, some brilliant but briefless
Templar. He selected, we are to believe, such a nominal
and pretended author for his work that the deception
must have been transparent. Shakespeare's incom-
petence for the part assigned to him could not have
been hidden for an hour ; and Bacon's attempt to deceive
the public would have failed, with disastrous results to

his own reputation for wisdom and adroitness. He would have succeeded only in creating a scandal, in which his enemies, who were numerous and unsparing, would have taken undisguised delight. There was then a fashion of writing news-letters to friends abroad or in the country, containing the latest talk of London, and serving in place of newspapers. Several collections of such letters have been preserved, and if the Baconian theory were true, we might have expected to find in them some such passage as this : " News have I none, save of Mr. Attorney Bacon, that hath writ plays which he daily acted by Burbage and his men. But his plays will Mr. Attorney not own nor avouch for his, professing to all men that they be writ by one Shakespeare, a lewd and idle fellow from the town of Stratford-upon-Avon, where the darkness of ignorance doth cover the earth. How Mr. Attorney will in this wise beguile the world with a saucy jape ye well may marvel ; but all men do laugh at his roguish devices."

The Baconians, none the less, suppose that the secret actually was kept ; that the public never suspected Shakespeare or guessed at Bacon ; that the conspiracy was perfectly successful, and was never unveiled until more than three hundred years had elapsed. The people of the sixteenth century, it may be said with very great confidence, were not so guileless. Those who attribute to them such childlike innocence know little of that age, —its subtlety, its intrigues, its spying, and its suspiciousness. Had the attention of the Government been turned to the matter—which would not have been improbable,

for Bacon had rivals and enemies in very high places,—
the secret service which had been brought to perfec-
tion by Sir Francis Walsingham, and had unmasked
the darkest conspiracies against the Crown, would
speedily have solved the more humble mystery of the
Globe.

Bacon made the position still more difficult by his
choice of confederates, and the wide extension he gave
to the plot. Prudence would have suggested that the
fewer persons he admitted to his confidence the better ;
but Bacon took a reckless delight in extending his opera-
tions and bringing in a small army of confederates.
Those who were initiated into the secret, and could
not have been excluded from it, were at first William
Shakespeare himself, Richard Burbage, and all the
members of the theatrical company,—John Heming,
Henry Condell, William Kemp, Augustine Phillips,
Richard Cowley, Lawrence Fletcher, Robert Armin,
Thomas Pope, Christopher Beeston, John Underwood,
John Lowin, and Joseph Taylor. But the plot thick-
ened, and Bacon soon admitted behind the scenes an
array of authors and publishers.

One of these accomplices was Richard Field, whose
name has been mentioned more than once in this work.
Field was born in Stratford where his father was a
tanner ; he came up to London, and entered into business
as a publisher. From his press in the Blackfriars came
the two poems, *Venus and Adonis* and *Lucrece*, each with
its dedication to Lord Southampton signed by William
Shakespeare. We are now to suppose that Bacon was

the real author ; that Shakespeare did not and could
not write them. Richard Field must have been well
aware of all this. He knew much more about Stratford,
his native place, than modern research has ever been
able to reveal. He had seen the ditches and drains which
figure in Baconian polemic ; they may have been
numerous near his father's yard ; and he was well
acquainted with the illiteracy : he was himself a sample
of it. He knew from whom he had obtained the manuscripts ; and knew that his fellow-townsman, whose
name he allowed to appear in the volumes as that of
the author, was a mere pretender. Richard Field at
least cannot have been a Stratfordian, although he gave
himself out for one. He was in the secret. He was a
member of the inner brotherhood.

Other publishers soon added themselves to the growing band of pretended Stratfordians and actual Baconians.
From time to time Bacon allowed one of his plays to
be printed, with the injunction that the name of William
Shakespeare should appear in the title page. A series
of small volumes appeared, each containing a single play ;
a list of them follows, to which the attention of the reader
is directed. It gives the title page in each case, with
the name of the author to whom the work is ascribed,
the publisher and the date :—

The Tragedy of King Richard the Second. By William
Shakespeare. Printed by Valentine Sims for Andrew Wise.
1598.
The Tragedy of King Richard the Third. By William Shakespeare. Printed by Thomas Creed for Andrew Wise. 1598.

Love's Labour's Lost. Newly corrected and augmented by W. Shakespeare. Imprinted at London by W. W. for Cuthbert Burby. 1598.

The History of Henry the Fourth. Newly corrected by W. Shakespeare. Printed by S. S. for Andrew Wise. 1599.

The Second Part of Henry the Fourth. Written by William Shakespeare. Printed by V. S. for Andrew Wise and William Aspley. 1600.

The Merchant of Venice. Written by William Shakespeare. Printed by J. R. for Thomas Heyes. 1600.

A Midsummer Night's Dream. Written by William Shakespeare. Imprinted at London for Thomas Fisher. 1600.

Much Ado about Nothing. Written by William Shakespeare. Printed by V. S. for Andrew Wise and William Aspley. 1600.

The Tragical History of Hamlet, Prince of Denmark. By William Shakespeare. Printed by J. R. for N. L. 1604.

The Tragedy of Hamlet, Prince of Denmark. By William Shakespeare. Printed for John Smethwick. 1611.

Mr. William Shakespeare, his *True Chronicle History of King Lear and his three Daughters.* Printed for Nathaniel Butter. 1608.

The History of Troilus and Cressida. Written by William Shakespeare. Imprinted by G. Eld for R. Bonian and H. Walley. 1609.

The Tragedy of Othello. Written by William Shakespeare. Printed by N. O. for Thomas Walkley. 1622.

Several natural reflections are suggested by this catalogue. We may notice the unanimity of the publishers in ascribing these works to William Shakespeare, and the astonishing variety in the names of the publishers themselves. Orthodox scholars find it all very simple ; the publishers issued the books as Shakespeare's, because they knew that he was the author, as any publisher may issue any book. The Baconians see behind it all the Prospero of the immense felt hat, waving his wand, directing and inspiring, sending an Ariel to printers' offices on mysterious errands, involving himself in what he thought an impenetrable haze. And yet he was running the gravest risks to his incognito. To select one publisher, and one alone, as the trustee of his secret, would have seemed a wise precaution ; but Bacon scattered it carelessly abroad in Fleet Street and St. Paul's Churchyard. Andrew Wise, Cuthbert Burby, William Aspley, Thomas Heyes, Thomas Fisher, John Smethwick, Nathaniel Butter, Richard Bonian, Henry Walley and Thomas Walkley were also of the inner brotherhood, unless we suppose that they saw nothing strange in the attribution of the plays, to Shakespeare, and were artless Stratfordians of the early prime.

It was in 1621 that the great disaster of Bacon's life took place. He was accused of accepting bribes in the administration of justice ; tried before the House of Lords and found guilty. A severe sentence was passed on him ; he was fined £40,000, imprisoned in the Tower of London during the King's pleasure, and declared for ever incapable of any office, place, or employment in the State. Some mitigation was indeed made to the unfortunate Lord Chancellor. King James remitted the fine, and ordered his release from the Tower ; but none the less his enemies had triumphed ; his day of greatness was over ; he had fallen like Lucifer, son of the morning. With a constancy and courage which we cannot but admire, Bacon retired to his private house,

and resumed his literary labours.   Many years before he
had published his *Advancement of Learning* in English.   He now resolved to rewrite the work in Latin,
with much augmentation, and toiled over it during
1622 and 1623, publishing it in October of the latter
year.

But now, under Baconian auspices, we have to add
a new chapter to the history of his literary works.   The
De Augmentis Scientiarum, a study which required severe
thought and prolonged concentration of mind, was not
the only project that occupied him during 1622 and 1623.
He resolved also to issue a complete edition of his
dramatic compositions.   He sat down and wrote a letter
which began, " Good Master Heming," and sent it by
a sure hand to the residence of the player in Alderman-
bury.   In this document, which unfortunately has not
been preserved, Bacon suggested that the time had now
come for the issue of all his comedies, histories and
tragedies in one volume, and begged that Master Heming
and Master Condell would see to it.   They did so ; and
towards the end of 1623 the English public had two
remarkable works placed before it, fresh from the press.
One was a treatise in Latin, learned, abstract and pro-
foundly thought out, on knowledge and the methods
of its attainment.   The other was a book of plays,
humorous, imaginative and tragic, containing the jests
of Falstaff, the melancholy of Hamlet, the grief and rage
of Othello ; and both—although the public never guessed
it—came from the same pen, and were the creations of
the same mind.

As publishers of the Folio, Bacon, or the Ariel who attended him, chose Isaac Jaggard and Edward Blount; who also accepted, or pretended to accept, the ascription of the authorship to William Shakespeare. Bacon, or his Ariel, also arranged for the poems in honour of William Shakespeare by Ben Jonson and Leonard Digges. He did something more extraordinary still. He caused the portrait of William Shakespeare to be prefixed to the volume. Bacon is thus the only poet known to history who published his works with the portrait of another man, an obscure and illiterate contemporary, as that of the author. But the grave statesman and philosopher was now in lighter vein, and as frolicsome and freakish as the Puck of his own youthful imagination. He desired to mislead his readers, and showed some ingenuity by the device ; we almost wonder how he came to think of it.

According to an inscription beneath the portrait itself, it was engraved by Martin Droeshout, an artist of Flemish descent ; it was an early effort, for Droeshout was then about twenty-two years old. In some Baconian circles there is a suggestion that it was deliberately faked, and had one sleeve turned round at the shoulder ; in order either to give the pretender a ridiculous air, and hint at his unreality, or to suggest that he was, like Cerberus, two gentlemen rolled into one. Whatever the motive for the faking may have been, the theory involves an assumption that the young artist, Martin Droeshout, had also been taken behind the scenes. The company of the elect continues to grow. But this time Bacon has extended his confidence with surprising recklessness, and surely for a very small object.

The deception which culminated in the publication of the Folio had already been continued with quiet persistence for thirty years, and had involved, as we have seen, much false statement and much connivance by very many people. There were not then all the means of recording facts which now exist, there were no newspapers, no magazines, no reviews. But London was a small city : men of letters congregated together in places of common resort ; information passed freely about. In books of occasional verse, in prose tracts and small treatises which flowed from the press, many allusions to Shakespeare and his works have been traced. Everywhere the story is the same ; it is Shakespeare who is admired and celebrated ; Bacon, in connection with the plays, is unknown, unheard of, undreamed of, passed over in total silence. The unanimity is perfect.

Extracts from the authors of the time are worth presenting. Prominence may be given to Francis Meres, a learned and thoughtful writer. Meres was just a year younger than Shakespeare, and was educated at Pembroke College, Cambridge. He became rector of a parish in Rutlandshire, where a great part of his life was spent ; but before his retirement thither had mingled in literary circles, and himself published several works. In 1598 appeared his *Palladis Tamia* which contains a critical essay on the English poets of the time. The passages on Shakespeare, in his elegant and Euphuistic manner, run as follows :—

" As the soul of Euphorbus was thought to live in Pytho-goras, so the sweet, witty soul of Ovid lives in mellifluous and honey-tongued Shakespeare,—witness his *Venus and Adonis*, his *Lucrece*, his sugared Sonnets among his private friends.

" As Plautus and Seneca are accounted the best for Comedy and Tragedy among the Latins, so Shakespeare among the English is the most excellent in both kinds for the stage. For Comedy witness his *Gentlemen of Verona*, his *Errors*, his *Love's Labour's Lost*, his *Love's Labour's Won*, his *Midsummer Night's Dream*, and his *Merchant of Venice* ; for Tragedy his *Richard the Second*, *Richard the Third*, *Henry the Fourth*, *King John*, *Titus Andronicus*, and his *Romeo and Juliet*.

" As Epius Stolo said that the Muses would speak with Plautus' tongue, if they would speak Latin, so I say that the Muses would speak with Shakespeare's fine-filed phrase if they would speak English."

Shakespeare's Sonnets had not yet been published, and Francis Meres could have seen them only in manuscript.

William Camden is another witness,—a man of infinite learning and industry, who had studied at Oxford in his youth, and in later life founded a Professorship there ; had been Headmaster of Westminster ; and at his death was buried in the Poets' Corner, where his monument may still be seen. Concerning Shakespeare he had special means of information. When the poet obtained confirmation of his coat-of-arms, it was to Camden, then acting as Clarencieux Herald, that the application was made. It then became his duty to investigate the case, to inform himself about Shakespeare's parentage, means, reputation, position in society, and eligibility for such a grant, which was not lightly given.

Camden knew what Shakespeare's family and ante-cedents were, and what manner of man Shakespeare himself was.   From him at least we may look for candour and accuracy ; and Camden has included William Shakes-peare by name amongst—his own words are quoted—the " most pregnant wits of these our times, whom suc-ceeding ages may justly admire."

Baconism, once more, has only one reply.   Camden is trying to beguile us.   Like Meres, he says " Shakes-peare " and he means " Bacon."   He also has joined the plot ; and we can but ask in astonishment what such a man is doing *dans cette galère.*

Another classical scholar, Gabriel Harvey, may also be quoted.   Harvey is well known as a friend of Edmund Spenser, and was a familiar figure in the Cambridge of Elizabeth.   He was a Fellow of Pembroke, and lectured as Professor of Rhetoric in the Public Schools.   Harvey's scholarly interests were not confined to classics alone. He eagerly discussed the work of his friend Spenser, in the letters which he exchanged with him, and was closely in touch with literary circles.   It was his practice to annotate his books with marginal reflections ; and not a few of them still survive with such notes in his clean and beautiful hand.   In his copy of Chaucer he set down some remarks on English poetry, from which the following is extracted :—

" The younger sort takes much delight in Shakespeare's *Venus and Adonis* ; but his *Lucrece* and his *Tragedy of Hamlet,*

Prince of Denmark have it in them to please the wiser sort."

The Cambridge Professor might indeed have said more about his illustrious contemporary ; but he has said enough for the present purpose. Gabriel Harvey is also among the Stratfordians. We may wonder whether he murmured to himself, as he sat in his study with a quill pen in his fingers : " Not Shakespeare's *Hamlet*, i' faith, but Bacon's *Hamlet*, though I may not say so." But the note was written for his own eyes alone, and Harvey could not have imagined that it would be found and published some centuries after he had passed away from the earth.

That Shakespeare was known as the author of his works to scholars and University men is apparent. His lack of an academic degree, and limited training at Stratford, seemed to them to be no obstacle, and raised no questioning in the minds of Leonard Digges, William Camden, Francis Meres and Gabriel Harvey.

Another fragment of University evidence may be found in the curious play entitled *The Return from Parnassus*, written at Cambridge, and performed by the students of St. John's College in 1601. It is an entertaining work, abounding in humour, satire and touches of contemporary manners. A familiar type of Elizabethan appears in several scenes, one Gullio, an affected fine gentleman. He has been a traveller, claims to have studied at the University of Padua, to have fought many duels and had many prosperous love affairs, and to be well versed in French, Italian and Spanish. Gullio raves about poetry, and has an endless flow of quotation, the poet whom he admires above all others being Mr. Shakespeare.

When Gullio enters, one of the other characters, Ingenioso, a Cambridge scholar, exclaims in alarm :—

" We shall have nothing but pure Shakespeare and shreads of poetry that he has gathered at the theatres."

Gullio immediately justifies these forebodings. He announces that compared with his mistress, Antony's Cleopatra was a black-browed milkmaid, and Helen a dowdy ; and declaims a stanza from *Venus and Adonis*. He then remembers the business which has brought him. New Year's Day approaches ; he would fain bestow a gift upon his mistress,—not a jewel, which is a common-place affair, but a copy of verses. Being himself employed in weighty matters, he invites Ingenioso to compose the poem, and afterwards he will peruse, polish and correct it. It is agreed that Ingenioso shall write several pieces on approbation, and that they shall be in the manner of Chaucer, Spenser and Mr. Shakespeare. Gullio does not leave it in doubt which of them he is likely to prefer :—

" Marry, I think I shall entertain these verses which run like these :
    Even as the sun with purple clouded face
    Had ta'en his last leave on the weeping morn.
O sweet Mr. Shakespeare ! I'll have his picture in my study at the court."

In a later scene Ingenioso reads the imitations of Chaucer,

Spenser and Shakespeare, which he has composed. The first two are summarily rejected, and Gullio accepts the lines in the Shakespearian vein.

" Ay, marry, sir, these have some life in them ! Let this duncified world esteem of Spenser and Chaucer, I'll worship sweet Mr. Shakespeare, and to honour him will lay his *Venus and Adonis* under my pillow, as we read of one (I do not well remember his name, but I am sure he was a King), slept with Homer under his bed's head."

The Return from Parnassus is a satirical comedy, and Gullio is a foolish person ; the enthusiasm of the young for Shakespeare's amorous verses is made the theme of jest ; but none the less the author, another scholar of Cambridge, adds his testimony to that of Meres, Digges, Camden and Harvey. He has no doubt that Shakespeare actually was the poet who composed *Venus and Adonis* and *Romeo and Juliet*. It has not occurred to him that a man from a country grammar school could not have written such works at all.

A great part of the play is concerned with the adventures of two unfortunate graduates, who are learning by sad experience how little is to be gained in this harsh world by a University education. They are in dire poverty ; try one profession after another in the hope of earning a livelihood, without success ; and at last bethink them of acting. The company they wish to join is that of which Shakespeare is a member. Burbage and Kemp are brought in person on the Cambridge stage, impersonated by two undergraduates, and consider their application for admission.   Burbage is affable and good-natured ; scholars, he remarks, have often a good conceit in a part ; a little teaching will mend their faults ; and they may be able, perhaps, to help the company by writing plays themselves.   Kemp, however, takes up a hostile attitude.   In his opinion scholars are seldom good performers ; and, as for writing plays, there is no need for academic graduates when they have Shakespeare himself among them.

> " Few of the University men pen plays well.   They smell too much of that writer Ovid, and that writer Metamorphosis, and talk too much of Proserpina and Jupiter.   Why ! here's our fellow Shakespeare puts them all down, aye, and Ben Jonson, too."

In actual truth Shakespeare himself is not exempt from the reproach which Kemp, the humorist of the company, is made to level at University men.   He also has studied his *Metamorphoses* ; he talks of Jupiter freely enough ; and in the most beautiful passage in *Winter's Tale* he has something to say of Proserpina :—

> " O Proserpina,
> For the flowers now that frighted thou let'st fall
> From Dis's waggon ! "

But, none the less, the evidence of the University wit who wrote *The Return from Parnassus* is of no small importance.   *Our fellow Shakespeare* has a plain meaning in Elizabethan English,—Shakespeare our partner and colleague.   The author of the play, and the academic world at Cambridge in which he lived, accepted Shakespeare the dramatist as identical with Shakespeare the actor.

The Baconian can explain these things only by falling back on his theory of a plot. The Cambridge don who wrote *The Return from Parnassus* was in the secret ; when he said Shakespeare, he meant Bacon ; when Gullio exclaims, " O sweet Mr. Shakespeare, I'll have his picture in my study," he really means, " O sweet Mr. Bacon, I'll have *his* picture in my study," and the Cambridge audience understood as much.

The plot ramifies, and it becomes hard to trace it through all its wanderings. Other men of letters add their contribution, John Davies, John Weever, Richard Carew, John Bodenham, Edmund Bolton, Richard Barnfield, John Webster, Thomas Freeman, Edmund Howes,—all of whom speak of Shakespeare as the author of the plays and poems at dates within his own lifetime. Bacon and his hidden agents have brought together a small army of confederates—actors, publishers, poets, dramatists, critics. We have now to add that these willing helpers also included three members of the House of Lords.

It has been said that the Folio of 1623 was dedicated by Heming and Condell to the Earl of Pembroke and his younger brother, the Earl of Montgomery. Those noblemen were chosen, not only for their distinguished rank and position at Court, but because they frequented the theatre, and had both admired the plays and favoured the poet himself. Heming and Condell thus write :—

" But since your Lordships have been pleased to think these trifles something heretofore, and have prosecuted both them and their author living with so much favour ; we hope that, they outliving him, and he not having the fate, common with some, to be executor to his own writings, you will use the like indulgence toward them, you have done unto their parent."

These proceedings offer no difficulty to the Stratfordian, but they involve the Baconian in serious embarrassment. For him the dedication is entirely bogus.   The author of the plays contained in the book was not, as Heming and Condell asserted, dead, but alive and well ; and he was not the William Shakespeare whose name they placed on the title page, and for whose works and memory they invoked the favour of the two Earls. What did Lord Pembroke and Lord Montgomery think of it all ?   Were they really deceived, and did they believe in the author-ship of Shakespeare,—whom, as Heming and Condell inform us, they had personally known ?   Or were they offended by this attempt to associate their names with that of an impostor, although there is no record of any protest or repudiation ?   Or were they also in the secret of Bacon's authorship, and aiding him—at some sacrifice to their dignity—to cover his tracks ?

The case of Lord Southampton is much stranger. He was deeply involved in Bacon's mystery, a member of the inner circle of the inner brotherhood. And yet Bacon prosecuted him for High Treason.

It was to Lord Southampton that *Venus and Adonis* was dedicated in 1593, and the *Rape of Lucrece* in 1594. Baconians are agreed that the letters of dedication signed

" William Shakespeare " were actually written by Francis
Bacon, and express *his* feelings of devotion to the young
Earl. Southampton must have known as much. He
must have been aware that there was no William Shakespeare in the business, and that the love expressed for
him was Francis Bacon's love, however strangely conveyed.

A few years later the Earl of Essex makes his attempt
to cause a rising in the city, and drew Southampton, his
intimate friend, with him into the design. The rebellion
was easily suppressed and Essex and Southampton were
brought to trial. The result was never in doubt ; Essex
and Southampton were both convicted and sentenced to
death. Bacon had been a friend of Essex, from whom
he had received many favours, but now forsook him,
and took part in compassing his destruction. He
appeared as Counsel for the Crown, and did not spare
the accused. Here is an extract from his speech against
them :—

" Neither is it any point of law, as my Lord Southampton
would have it believed, that condemns them of treason, but
it is apparent in common sense. To take secret counsel, to
execute it, to run together in numbers armed with weapons
—what can be the excuse ? Warned by the Lord Keeper,
by a herald, and yet persist. Will any simple man take this
to be less than treason."

In itself this argument is well-founded ; but it was
all the more deadly for the prisoners. Essex was
beheaded. Southampton, who was considered the less
guilty of the two, escaped with his life ; but was left

imprisoned in the Tower. After the accession of James he was released and taken into the favour of the new sovereign. Bacon then wrote to him a dreary letter of apology and protestation ; seeking to disarm his resentment, but admitting that the Earl might be unwilling to see him, and might pay no heed to his declarations of friendship. It is not recorded that Southampton sent any reply.

The time came when the parts were reversed, and Bacon was himself on trial, with Southampton among his prosecutors. When it was suspected that he had degraded the office of Lord Chancellor by corrupt practices, committees were appointed by the House of Lords to investigate the charges and collect the evidence. Southampton was a member of one of the committees, and took an active part in the proceedings of the House. After Bacon had been condemned, there was some delay in enforcing the judgment, and Southampton rose to protest : " That the Lord Chancellor is not yet gone to the Tower, and the world may think our sentence is in vain."

These are the occasions in history when the names of Bacon and Southampton are associated. We are to believe, if Baconism is true, that when they thus appeared alternately as accuser and accused when Bacon prosecuted Southampton on a capital charge, when Southampton left his cell, burning with resentment against the false friend who had laboured to place him there, and when he joined with the Lords in preparing his ruin and disgrace,—they were none the less united in a common secret, and were conspiring together to delude the public by a literary fraud.

And we may ask again, in no small astonishment, by what motive these mysterious transactions are explained. Why did Lord Southampton accept a bogus dedication? Why did Ben Jonson clothe himself in lies as with a garment? Why did Camden, Harvey, Digges and Meres join to swell the chorus of untruth? Why did every writer of that age who has mentioned the matter at all ascribe the plays to Shakespeare, and to Shakespeare alone?

It cannot have been that all were paid for their assistance. Bacon was not rich, lived beyond his income, and was constantly in pecuniary embarrassment. By what means did he bribe the wealthy Earls of Southampton and Pembroke? And it cannot have been from a simple and childlike kindness, a disinterested desire to do Bacon a service. He was not personally popular, and at certain times his unpopularity was great. He also had enemies who would have welcomed any opportunity of exposing the intrigue had they come to suspect its existence. Many keen eyes followed his actions. The pathway to success at Tudor and Stuart Courts was a slippery one; and there is a fierce light which beats upon aspirants to legal promotion.

At one dangerous moment, before his final fall, when the favour of King James seemed averted from him, his enemies were preparing to rush upon their prey. A friend wrote from Court to warn him of his peril, and thus faithfully exposed the situation :—

K

" It is too common in every man's mouth in Court that your greatness shall be abated, and as your tongue hath been a razor to some, so shall theirs be to you."

When the Court was thus in excitement, and men were seeking for some weapon of scandal and offence, they would have welcomed with avidity the revelation that Bacon had been engaged for twenty years in writing plays for a theatre and sheltering himself behind the name of one of the actors. The jests and triumph of his enemies would have known no bounds.

The most dangerous of his opponents was the Lord Chief Justice, Sir Edward Coke. The feud was one of long standing. They had been rivals in their profession from their youth, and rivals for the favour of the Crown. They had been rivals in love, or rather in the pursuit of wealth by means of matrimony. Coke carried off the opulent widow, and Bacon afterwards revenged himself by an ill-judged interference in his domestic affairs. We have on record, in Bacon's hand, the narrative of a stormy interview between these eminent jurists. " The less you speak of your own greatness, the more I will think of it," said Bacon ; " I have been your better, and may be again." Coke retorted, less epigrammatically, by asking his antagonist to mind his own business, and hinting at some offence for which Bacon deserved to be outlawed. An allusion to stage-plays would have been more telling. The Chief Justice entertained a strong Puritanic aversion to the drama, and had the faintest whisper of Bacon's theatrical dealings ever reached his ears, would not have failed to note it. But

Coke never dreamed that his rival, whom he watched with sleepless suspicion and with one of the most acute minds in England, was actually a dramatist in disguise.

Bacon thus succeeded in his perilous undertaking. He and his allies, men of the most varied rank, many of them strangers to each other,—actors, publishers, poets, scholars, courtiers, noblemen,—combined to preserve the secret inviolate. They completely deceived those around them ; and the deception went down unsuspected to posterity. For Bacon was not content to hide his authorship from his contemporaries alone : he was equally anxious to escape from posthumous fame as a dramatic poet. Another man might have been willing that the truth should be divulged after his death, and having denied himself the glory of his own poetic genius in his lifetime, might have desired at least to obtain recognition in years to come. Bacon was not indifferent to such perpetuity of renown. In his will he bequeathed his name and memory " to foreign nations and the next ages "; but made no claim to the poetical works which alone would have immortalized him. He requested Sir John Constable and Sir William Boswell to act as his literary executors, instructing them to deposit copies of all his writings in certain libraries which he named ; but these gentlemen did not attempt after his decease to vindicate his right to his own dramatic compositions.

Thus the poetical works of Bacon, which had been published as those of an obscure impostor, were abandoned without a word of protest. Knowing himself to be the greatest of dramatic poets, he was content that the world should never know,—with strange indifference to the honour and fame that reward " the feverish exercise of the imagination," considered by Sir Walter Scott to be the most arduous of all forms of labour. His dramas had cost him many years of toil, with all the strain upon the faculties and feelings demanded by poetic creation. He asked no recompense but the opportunity of conferring perpetual glory upon another man, to whom he was bound by no ties and to whom he owed less than nothing. History records no other example of such self-abnegation.

His friends and followers honoured his wishes ; and years after Bacon had been laid in St. Michael's Church, they continued to propagate the fable he had taught them. It descended undetected for centuries ; and for centuries our greatest poet was deprived of the honour which might have been his, had he but put forth his hand to take it.

Such are the difficulties that beset us, and the maze of complications in which our feet must wander, when we make a problem of Shakespeare's authorship, and seek refuge in the Baconian solution.

VI

SCHOLARSHIP

I

The literary historians of the last generation had evolved no consistent theory of Shakespeare and his environment, and left an obvious gap between them, which they had no means of bridging. On one hand they magnified the splendour of the Elizabethan Age. It was a time of inspired patriotism and triumphant expansion of mind. Great poets adorned it, and manifested the glory of their genius. But alongside of this conception and never co-related with it, was another, which was derived from a different source. The modern world was only too conscious of its own superiority, only too much inspired by the idea of Progress, which made all former times seem barbarous and ignorant. To be modern was to be enlightened and civilized, advancing on the highway to still greater enlightenment and civilization. The English society of three hundred years ago was painted in darker contrast than the true colours warranted ; its crudity of mind and manners, its barbarism even, and savagery were particularly emphasized.

From this slighting of the past arose a belief—assumed rather than implied—that the men of that time were our inferiors in native intelligence as well as in accumulated knowledge, which they certainly were not, and a failure to perceive what is evident to minute students of the period,—that the Englishmen of Elizabeth's time were in truth the inheritors of a very ancient and mature civilization, a practised sagacity, and a dignified code of manners. They were made to appear picturesque barbarians. Finally, when conceptions which were in themselves contradictory were brought into open conflict, it became impossible to explain where the great poets of the Elizabethan Age could possibly have come from, and how they found a public to read their books or fill their theatres.

Yet to a dramatic poet like Shakespeare the immediate appreciation of his contemporaries is as the breath of life. He cannot ignore the men around him, and work in his study, contemplating a fit audience, though few, or looking for recognition as Bacon did " to foreign countries and the next ages." He is dependent on conditions which he cannot ignore. He must have actors who possess sufficient intelligence and refinement of feeling to enter into the spirit of his works, and interpret them with sympathy ; and he must have an audience which is ready and eager to listen. If these conditions are not fulfilled, nothing can be done. The wheels of his chariot refuse to go round. Without the competent actors and the willing and comprehending audience he cannot exist.

And the conditions of dramatic representation are such that the author cannot take the risk of boring his audience or talking over their heads. A preacher may perplex and weary his hearers, and suffer no inconvenience ; a lecturer may do so, with no result but a silent and unobtrusive movement towards the door ; but a dramatist who does so is in danger of immediate interruption. He must not allow his hold upon the attention of the spectators to relax for a moment ; and, if he fails to keep it, they may—according at least to the ancient manners of the theatre—express their disapproval at the failure of the entertainment in a very noisy fashion. An unsuccessful play was still hissed down vigorously in the days of Kemble and Kean ; and the curtain might fall for the last time long before the final act was reached.

The Elizabethan audience certainly practised the art of hissing down a play which failed to interest them. Shakespeare himself expresses the hope that one of his works may " scape the serpent's tongue." Spenser speaks of cries and uproar—" Such as the troubled Theatres oft-times annoys "—and Leonard Digges tells us that, whilst the public listened with wonder and ravishment to *Julius Cæsar*, it would not tolerate Ben Jonson's tedious tragedy of *Catiline*. Noisy interruption was ready and prompt in Elizabethan theatres when the play proved wearisome.

The art of the drama is that now known as " getting it over the footlights " ; and the first condition of that art is to avoid presenting the spectators with anything which they do not understand. The dramatist cannot afford to let their attention flag ; still less to repel them by unfamiliar allusions or quotations in an unintelligible language. That Shakespeare knew his public and how to address it must be allowed ; his immense and immediate popularity is sufficient evidence. Let us consider what he expected of his auditors, and what assumptions he made when composing a drama.

He took for granted that they were interested in poetry, and would listen, not only with toleration but with rapt interest, to the long speeches of Jacques, Hamlet and Macbeth. He took for granted that they were attracted by allusions to classical history and classical mythology ; and he took for granted that they would instantly understand phrases in Latin, French and Italian, and would be pleased by hearing them. If Shakespeare had not made all these assumptions, neither the long poetical speeches, nor the classical allusions, nor the scraps of Latin, French and Italian, would ever have found a place in his works.

He even goes beyond isolated phrases in foreign languages. In *Henry V* there are several scenes at the French Court and on the field of Agincourt where more French is spoken than English. When Shakespeare composed them, he must have had, like all dramatists, the theatre before his mind's eye ; and must have reckoned on the reception which his scenes would meet with. He must have known that the dialogues in French would be immediately intelligible to most of his audience, and would afford them amusement. Nowadays an English drama

containing snatches of dialogue in French is a thing
unheard of ; and when *Henry V* is revived the producers
are shy of the French passages, and cut them down or
omit them altogether. The only inference we can draw
is that French was much more generally understood in
London in Shakespeare's day than it is at the present
time. Had it been otherwise, the French dialogue
would have broken the spell ; the audience would have
been puzzled and irritated, and would have shown its
disapproval ;—and Shakespeare would have foreseen all
this, and would not have written in French. Obviously
he had in view a public which he expected to understand
and enjoy such passages. Nearly a century afterwards
when the Popish Plot was in agitation, a man named
Staley was arrested for some treasonable expressions
which he was said to have uttered in French in an eating-
house in Covent Garden. He defended himself by
arguing " how improbable it was that in a public-house
he should talk such things, with so loud a voice as to
be heard in the next room, in a quarter of the town where
almost everybody understood French." [1]

Small fragments about the behaviour of Elizabethan audiences have been collected, and attempts have been made to
piece them together, and thus to reconstruct for modern
eyes an afternoon at the Globe or the Blackfriars. But the
most vital evidence, the key to the problem, is to be found
in the plays themselves. No dramatist who has had a
long and intimate association with the stage ever goes
contrary to the tastes of his public. Shakespeare was

[1] Burnet's *History of My Own Time*, Chap. IX.

by far the most popular dramatist of his time.   Leonard
Digges informs us, in the lines already mentioned, that
the public flocked to his theatre and listened in spell-bound
silence :—

> " Oh ! how the audience
> Were ravished ; with what wonder they went thence "—

when Brutus and Cassius were seen at parley, their
swords half drawn, when Falstaff and his company
appeared, or Beatrice and Benedick, or the cross-gartered
gull Malvolio. The playwright who thus appealed to
them knew his public, and his sympathies and tastes
agreed with theirs. He gave them great poetry, because
he was a great poet, and because they also understood
and loved great poetry. He gave them classical mythology, because both poet and audience delighted in it ;
and he gave them fragments of Latin, French and Italian
because the knowledge of those languages was a common
and popular thing.

" But what then of the groundlings," it may be asked,
" and did not Shakespeare address his plays to them ? "
Groundlings there certainly were,—the spectators of the
poorer class who stood in the cheapest part of the house
where no seats were provided ; and Shakespeare himself
says that they were for the most part able to appreciate
nothing in an actor's performance but " inexplicable
dumb shows and noise," the waving arms and the sten-
torian voice. But it was not to the groundlings that the
plays were addressed, and to offer what they might
desire was the last thing Shakespeare ever contemplated.

In the whole of his plays he mentions the groundlings but once, and only once, and then to condemn with much emphasis—" it offends me to the soul "—the conduct of actors who exaggerated their parts and ranted to please them. He would not have spoken of them from the stage with such open disdain had there been any cause to seek their approbation or dread their displeasure. His real public was the noblemen and courtiers, and members of learned professions, the prosperous citizens who thronged the house. The plays were intended for them, and the world is looked at from their point of view, which was also the poet's own. He intended his works for the same public for which Spenser wrote the *Faerie Queene* and Byrd and others composed their airs.

Such contemporary allusions to theatrical audiences as have been found are brief and fragmentary. The most interesting and valuable is that of a foreign observer, which has attracted singularly little attention, although it is many years since it was first brought to light.

About 1850 an aged gentleman died at Venice, the last of the house of Contarini, which had given eight Doges to the Republic. He bequeathed the papers of his family to the Library of St. Mark; and amongst them was found a series of letters written from London by Orazio Busino, who was chaplain to the Venetian Embassy in the time of James I. They are the work of a curious, lively and intelligent observer, extenuating nothing, and setting down nothing in malice. Orazio Busino, soon after his arrival in London, paid a visit

to one of the theatres, and thus recorded his impressions
in a letter written in December, 1617 :—

" The other day they resolved to take me to one of the
many theatres here in London, where comedies are recited ;
and there we saw the performance of a tragedy, which affected
me very little, chiefly because I cannot understand a single
word of English.   One could get some pleasure only by gazing
at the magnificent dresses of the reciters, and observing their
gestures and the various interludes of music, dancing, singing
and such-like things.   The best entertainment was to see and
contemplate so many noblemen so finely arrayed, that they
looked like so many princes, and listening with such silence
and respect.   And many honourable and fair ladies come
there with perfect freedom, and take their seats amongst the
men without hesitation."

It is unlucky that Busino does not name the place he
visited ; and it may have been one of the private theatres,
such as the Blackfriars, which was then in the possession
of Shakespeare's own company and was used by them in
the winter months.   The terms of the description indicate a building of some size, an elaborate entertainment,
and a very fashionable assembly.   One thing is certain ;—
through the eyes of the Venetian stranger we may see
the very audience for which Shakespeare wrote his plays,
and to whose judgment he appealed,—the noblemen
listening with such silence and respect—*con tanto silenzio
e modestia*—and the fair and honourable ladies who sat
among them.   It was for them that he designed his
Hamlet and *Othello*, his royal Richards and Henries, his
Rosalind, Beatrice and Viola.

II

In these remarks a degree of cultivation has been attributed to Shakespeare which is higher than many writers conceive he possessed. Evidence for its existence is to be found in the plays themselves. His plays are obviously the work of a man who had a very copious command of expressive language, a noble style, and an exquisite refinement of taste ; and none of these things is to be obtained by an author without an adequate acquaintance with other men's works. His plays have been minutely searched for traces of his reading ; but we cannot expect to find the whole compass of it represented there. Poetry may indicate something far short of a writer's actual acquirements. From the internal evidence of Gray's *Elegy in a Country Churchyard*, no one could guess that its author was one of the most learned men then living in Europe. Some allusions there are to Hampden, Cromwell and Milton ; but profound knowledge is not required to suggest such names. Wordsworth had not the erudition of Gray, but he was none the less a man of books. His library at Rydal Mount was dispersed long ago ; but a printed catalogue of it is extant. It contained nearly three thousand volumes, many of them covered with marginal annotations. Only the scantiest handful amongst them could be traced to his possession by the evidence of his own poetical works.

Shakespeare, even by the indications afforded in his plays, certainly read Latin, and was familiar with some

chosen authors, of whom the first in favour was Ovid ;
for Ovidian reminiscences are scattered in them with a
lavish hand. Four lines of Ovid are quoted in the
original in *The Taming of the Shrew*. The title page of
Shakespeare's first published poem, *Venus and Adonis*,
is likewise adorned with a citation from Ovid in the original
Latin. The material of the poem is also drawn from
Ovid ; so is that of *Lucrece*. The allusions to classical
mythology and legend which charmed Shakespeare's first
admirers in the theatre can be traced to the same source.

> " In such a night
> Medea gathered the enchanted herbs
> That did renew old Æson,"

says Lorenzo in *The Merchant of Venice*. The story of
Medea and how she renewed Æson's youth by her
enchantments, is found in the seventh book of the
Metamorphoses. Shakespeare was so interested in the
passage that he took from it likewise the image of Hecate,
goddess of witchcraft,—

> " And we fairies that do run
> By the triple Hecate's team,"—

and Medea's lines describing the potency of her spells,
which he transfers to Prospero. When he wrote *Midsummer Night's Dream* he was fresh from a recent and
delighted study of the *Metamorphoses* : its traces are
everywhere in the poem,—in the name of Titania, as well
as the allusion to Hecate, and the story of Pyramus and
Thisbe. Hermia swears love to Lysander :—

> " By Cupid's strongest bow
> By his best arrow with the golden head."

In Ovid we read that Cupid has two arrows :—

" that which causes love is of gold, and is bright with a sharp point : that which repels it is blunt, and has lead beneath the reed."

In the Induction to *The Taming of the Shrew*, Christopher Sly is invited to see a series of pictures presenting the loves of the gods, Daphne pursued by Apollo, and

> " Io, as she was a maid,
> And how she was beguiled and surprised,
> As lively painted as the deed was done."

Ovid in the *Metamorphoses* describes a similar series of pictures, woven in the web of Arachne. Autolycus in *Winter's Tale*, the snapper-up of unconsidered trifles, is an Ovidian figure, the son of Mercury, ingenious in every kind of theft. At the sheep-shearing feast, Perdita, the shepherdess, who is also a princess, cries :—

> " O Proserpina,
> For the flowers now that frighted thou let'st fall
> From Dis's waggon ! daffodils
> That come before the swallow dares, and take
> The winds of March with beauty ; violets dim,
> But sweeter than the lids of Juno's eyes
> Or Cytherea's breath."

The lines were suggested by Ovid, who describes how Proserpina when at play, plucking violets or white lilies, and filling her basket and bosom, was beheld, beloved and seized by Pluto. The frightened goddess called on her mother and her companions, and, as she tore her garments, the flowers fell from her loosened robes. Many such resemblances may be traced,—enough to show that the romantic Roman poet was known to Shakespeare almost by heart. In *Love's Labour's Lost* is the declaration, attributed to the learned and pedantic Holofernes, that for the elegancy, facility, and golden cadence of poesy, " Ovidius Naso was the man."

Even *Hamlet* is not without Ovidian reminiscence, although the tragic tone of the drama might have excluded them. There are two in the first act :—

> " In the most high and palmy state of Rome,
> A little ere the mightiest Julius fell,
> The graves stood tenantless and the sheeted dead
> Did squeak and gibber in the Roman streets."

The source of these lines is revealed in the last book of the *Metamorphoses*. And when the Ghost utters the words :—

> " And duller shouldst thou be than the fat weed
> That roots itself in ease on Lethe wharf,
> Wouldst thou not stir in this " ;

he alludes, as Ovid shows us, to the poppy,—" fecunda papavera florent." [1]

Plautus, as a writer of comedy, attracted Shakespeare no less ; and influenced the structure, manner, dialogue and choice of characters in his early works. The *Comedy*

---

[1] *Classical Mythology in Shakespeare*, by R. K. Root, New York, 1903.

of Errors is a free adaptation of one of the plays of Plautus. In *The Taming of the Shrew* the names of the two servants, Tranio and Grumio, are directly taken from another, the *Mostellaria* ; and the whole of that drama is visibly touched by Plautine methods. So is the *Two Gentlemen of Verona*, and so in a lesser degree are other works of the same kind. The affable and witty servants, who exchange jest and repartee with their masters, the Dromios, Grumio, Launce, and Launcelot Gobbo, reproduce a familiar type in Latin comedy ; the bragging and swaggering soldiers who are cowards at heart, Parolles, Pistol, and even Falstaff, may trace their ancestry to the same source ; the nurse in *Romeo and Juliet* resembles another stock figure of the Roman drama.

How Shakespeare accepted the methods of the Roman stage may also appear by some passages which have perplexed his commentators. In *The Taming of the Shrew* certain characters arrive by sea at Padua, having voyaged thither in a ship from Pisa. Lucentio and Tranio have already landed, and the former remarks :—

> " If, Biondello, thou wert come ashore,
> We could at once put us in readiness."

But Padua is an inland town ; and the way from Pisa to Padua is across the wide Lombard plain. The *Two Gentlemen of Verona* presents the same difficulty, the travellers voyaging in ships between Verona and Milan, which also are inland towns.

An explanation of these passages has been sought in geographical information about rivers and canals ; but

L

it is very wide of the mark. The theory has been stated more than once, and with much display of learning ; but it is evident that Shakespeare did not have rivers and canals in view. When the servant Speed, a jocular knave, is about to embark with his master, Proteus exclaims :—

"Go, go, begone, to save your ship from wrack,
    Which cannot perish having thee aboard,
    Being destined to a drier death on shore."

Only a voyage in the open sea could give occasion for shipwreck. In a later scene Launce is thus addressed by Panthino :—

" Launce, away, away, aboard ! Thy master is shipped, and thou art to post after with oars. . . . Away, ass, *you will lose the tide*, if you tarry any longer."

But Verona is far inland, and the Adige, which flows through it, is not a tidal stream. Their true source is to be found in Shakespeare's adoption of a conventional usage in Latin comedy. Plautus assumes the existence of a harbour behind the scenes, where his characters are supposed to disembark, the arrival by sea being nothing more than a symbol for the coming of a stranger who is not one of the group of characters inhabiting the town. Those who thus came from a distance entered the stage from one side, where the harbour was assumed to be ; those who arrived from streets or market-places within the city itself entering from the other. Following this convention Plautus, in the *Amphitruo*, has placed a harbour at Thebes, which is an inland city, like Verona and Padua. The reappearance of this device in Shakespeare indicates how familiar the Roman drama had become to his mind. In imaginative comedies such names as " Verona " and " Milan " have no real significance. They are merely designations given in different acts to the stage on which the performance takes place. Any names will serve the purpose.

Hamlet's favourite author is Juvenal ; and in his talk he easily falls into a Juvenalian vein. On entering with a book in his hand, poring over its pages, he is asked by Polonius,—" What do you read, my lord ? " Hamlet answers that the book is that of a *satirical rogue*, who dwells on the infirmities of age, saying that " old men have grey beards, that their faces are wrinkled ; their eyes purging thick amber and plum-tree gum ; and that they have a plentiful lack of wit, together with most weak hams." It is the Tenth Satire of Juvenal that Hamlet is reading when Polonius interrupts him ; and when in his talk with Ophelia, he rails against women, their vanity and affectation and use of cosmetics, he is drawing inspiration from the Sixth.

A familiar acquaintance with the Latin language, and with three or four favourite authors, was a common possession of educated men who had been to a Grammar School in their youth ; it could do nothing to set Shakespeare on a pedestal apart. The statement that he had no pretension to scholarship is relative to the standard of scholarship we set up. It was easily made in the seventeenth century, an age of laborious application and ponderous folios ; when ability to read Latin and some acquaintance with Ovid and Plautus, Virgil and Juvenal, seemed to professional scholars to be nothing more than the trivial rudiments of a schoolboy. Shakespeare might know Latin well enough, and read Ovid and Plautus ; and Jonson might none the less speak of his small Latin, and Fuller might say that he had little learning, and owed more to Nature than to Art. Shakespeare did not profess to be a scholar. He was an English gentleman of his time, and read the Latin poets for his own pleasure, as other English gentlemen did.

In his familiarity with modern languages Shakespeare again represents the educated public of his day. England was then more cosmopolitan and less insular or self-centred than it afterwards became. John Bull had not yet been invented ; the Englishman did not yet take pride in his own isolation. The popular enthusiasm, as Shakespeare's own plays abundantly testify, was all for travel, foreign fashions, and polyglot attainments. The highest commendation that can be given to a fashionable Sir Andrew is that he " speaks three or four languages word for word without book, and has all the good gifts of nature."   Even the outlaws in the *Two Gentlemen of Verona*, one of the earliest of Shakespeare's comedies, will not be satisfied until they have asked Valentine, " Have you the tongues ? " ; and on hearing his reply :—

> " My youthful travel therein made me happy,
>   Or else I often had been miserable,"

they elect him captain of their band,—apparently in all seriousness.

Shakespeare himself, however he may sometimes satirize the prevailing taste, had his own full share of it. Both Italian and French had become so familiar to his mind that he easily dropped into them, and expected his audience to do the same. The fine gentlemen in *The Taming of the Shrew* exchange greetings in fluent Tuscan, —*Con tutto il cuore, ben trovato*, says Petruchio ; and Hortensio answers, *Alla nostra casa ben venuto, molto honorato signor mio Petruchio.* But the clowns also have glimmerings of the foreign speech, and Bottom addresses the fairies as Signor, and Monsieur. At the present day we could not imagine a comedy presenting life in an English country town in which an innkeeper is supposed to talk Italian ; but in *The Merry Wives of Windsor* Shakespeare assigns it to the host of the Garter, who speaks of Slender as Cavaliere, and, having occasion to rebuke his servant, addresses him as *Varletto*. Pistol, a mere hanger-on of Falstaff's discreditable gang, has his Italian quotation. Christopher Sly, in the midst of his racy Stratford talk, calls himself *Cristofero*.

Attendance at a University was not needed for acquaintance with foreign tongues. A smattering might even be obtained at Stratford, where Shakespeare's son-in-law, Thomas Quiney, adorned the first page in his book of accounts, now in the archives of the town, with some lines of French. But the best place for such acquirement which could be found in England was London itself, with its foreign colonies and foreign teachers, and the influence of fashionable example ; and Shakespeare had hardly arrived there when he plunged into the stream of popular study.[1]

Richard Farmer's *Essay on the Learning of Shakespeare* was once accepted as the authoritative and final study of the subject, and its influence lingers to this day. Farmer disposed effectively of the contention that Shakespeare was a good Greek scholar ; but he carried the theory of his ignorance to ridiculous extremes. Modern languages he denied to Shakespeare altogether ; holding that he had no more French and Italian than a few phrases which he had found quoted in English books, or picked up in the course of conversation. The use of such phrases in English writers of the time, and in the conversation of the poet's friends, suggests a very general knowledge of modern languages ; from which Shakespeare, it is assumed, was excluded : he was the rare exception. In answer to the argument that he shows an acquaintance with the works of Rabelais,[2] which were still untranslated into English, Farmer retorts that he heard them talked about, the French original being then " in every one's hands,"—i.e. familiar to every one

[1] How far Shakespeare was acquainted personally with the foreign colonies in London is a curious question. In *Othello* he mentions a character called *Marcus Lucchese*, whose name very incidentally appears. There was then in real life an Italian bearing the name of Marco Lucchese. He was the proprietor of the Italian ordinary, or restaurant, and his establishment was frequented by Italian visitors to London. The identity of the names is suggestive.—*Modern Language Review*.

[2] Gargantua, *As You Like It*, III, ii.

except Shakespeare himself, who knew Rabelais only by report, unlike all his neighbours. Farmer thus assigns to the poet an education much below the average level of the society in which he moved ; but does not explain why a man possessing his intelligence should be found only in this position of mental inferiority.

That Shakespeare never graduated at Oxford or Cambridge is not of itself enough to set him down in the ranks of ignorance : creative energy, imaginative power, elevation of mind, and beauty of style may be possessed without a day spent within the walls of a University ; and so may all the signs of comprehensive reading. Illustration of these facts are abundant.

John Keats received what education he possessed in a private school, where he learned no Greek, but acquired Latin enough to read Ovid and to make a prose translation of the *Æneid*. At the age of sixteen he was apprenticed to a surgeon and apothecary, and thenceforth read, eagerly and widely, for himself in all manner of books. His poems display an intimate and loving acquaintance with classical mythology. Did we not know his history, it would be easy to argue that *Hyperion* and *Endymion*, the *Ode to a Grecian Urn* and the *Ode to Psyche* could only have been written by a University man.

Charles Dickens received a much more scanty education than Keats, and seems to have had no knowledge of Greek and Latin at all. Yet to call Dickens illiterate would be the merest misuse of language. We have in his own words this charming picture of the child who is afterwards to be a man of genius :—

" My father had left a small collection of books in a little room upstairs to which I had access (for it adjoined my own), and which nobody else in our house ever troubled. From that blessed little room, *Roderick Random*, *Peregrine Pickle*, *Humphrey Clinker*, *Tom Jones*, *The Vicar of Wakefield*, *Don Quixote*, *Gil Blas*, and *Robinson Crusoe* came out, a glorious host to keep me company. They kept alive my fancy, and my hope of something beyond that place and time,—they, and the *Arabian Nights*, and the *Tales of the Genii*—and did me no harm ; for, whatever harm was in some of them, was not there for me ; *I* knew nothing of it."

When his age was only ten the boy was taken from school, by the neglect and indifference of his parents, and sent to work in a dismal warehouse, where he toiled in helpless misery—it was the age of child labour— pasting labels on pots of blacking. " No words can express the secret agony of my soul," he says, " as I felt my early hopes of growing up to be a learned and distinguished man crushed in my breast." After two years of this weary drudgery he was sent once more to school, to a place called an Academy, kept by an ignorant and incompetent master ; he became a clerk in an attorney's office at fifteen ; then a newspaper reporter ; and at twenty-four conquered fame and fortune by the publication of the *Pickwick Papers*.

George Meredith knew nothing of Universities. He was the son of a tailor at Portsmouth ; spent a few years at a school in Germany at Neuwied on the Rhine ; and after his return to England became a clerk in a solicitor's office. Although he is so much nearer to our own time, his early life is almost as obscure as that of Shakespeare himself. His latest biographer admits that his first two years in London are a perfect blank.

In all essentials Meredith was a self-educated man, owing everything he possessed to his own reading and meditation. But in tone and feeling he is nothing if not aristocratic. It would not have been difficult to argue from his works, with their very rare and exquisite culture, that he had received the best education in England and led the most sheltered of lives.

Robert Louis Stevenson had no very regular or comprehensive education. He attended schools in Edinburgh, and fitfully visited classes in the University there. Greek he abandoned as hopeless; he had some Latin, but only for his own purposes, and read Livy in the South Seas. His biographer, Mr., now Sir, Graham-Balfour, writes :—

" As to his classics he was ignorant of Greek, and preferred the baldest of Bohn's translations to more literary versions that might come between him and the originals. His whole relation to Latin, however, was very curious and interesting. He had never mastered the grammar of the language, and to the end made the most elementary mistakes. Nevertheless he had a keen appreciation of the best authors, and, indeed, I am not sure that Virgil was not more to him than any other poet, ancient or modern."

Thomas Hardy spent his boyhood at elementary schools in country places, where he learned little more than his native language; and at the age of sixteen was apprenticed to an architect in Dorchester. He afterwards obtained some tuition in Latin and Greek from a friend. In *Tess of the D'Urbervilles* he quotes a phrase from the *Prometheus Bound* of Æschylus,—although Shakespeare's allusion to the *Ajax* of Sophocles has been thought to exclude him decisively from the authorship of the play in which it appears.

Keats, Dickens, Meredith, Stevenson and Hardy : these are distinguished names, and all are outside academic limits.   Yet no one would now treat their lack of University degrees as a matter of reproach, or a stumbling-block to their admirers.   They are moderns, and we look at them in the modern way.   But in the case of Shakespeare we are still under the influence of an obsolete mode of thought.   We still follow the tradition of the seventeenth century and the eighteenth ; we still look for an academic record and classical erudition, and make a great matter of their absence.   The old conception so plainly stated by David Hume,—that Shakespeare was a man " born in a rude age and educated in the lowest manner, without any instruction from the world or from books,"—still haunts discussion.   Baconians and academic Shakespearians here meet on common ground ; but soon their paths diverge.   Sometimes Shakespeare is peremptorily set aside.   There can be no difficulty about Marlowe, it is said : Marlowe was at Cambridge : but Shakespeare, who was not at either University, is merely beyond the pale.   Sometimes the ignorant professional playwright is saved at the last moment by the miracle of genius.

Residence at a University for a few years in youth is a very crude test of learning.   It would at once be fatal to Richard Baxter, who was never at Oxford or Cambridge.

" My faults," he said, " are no disgrace to any University, for I was of none ; I have little but what I had out of books, and inconsiderable helps of country tutors." Yet Richard Baxter was not an ignorant fellow. We do not know that Shakespeare would have profited greatly by a University course. He might have widened and deepened his Latin ; but that is not a certainty. It is not an uncommon experience that boys work hard and learn much at school, and profit little by their University days. Dr. Johnson told his friends " that his great period of study was from the age of twelve to eighteen," and that he read Latin with as much ease when he first went up to Oxford as he did in later life.

He might have learned Greek, but even that is not a certainty. In the age of Elizabeth it was possible to reside at a University for years, and leave it as a Master of Arts, without knowing a word of Greek. The established and prescribed studies were Logic and Philosophy ; to them all the energies of official instruction were devoted. Greek was introduced into Oxford by Linacre and Grocyn, and into Cambridge by Smith, Cheke, and Ascham,—names never to be mentioned without honour ; but after the first enthusiasm was over it greatly declined. By the middle of Elizabeth's reign a knowledge of Greek was the rare exception.[1] It was pursued by a few select spirits, but it formed no part of the prescribed course, and even the highest academic positions could be attained with little or none. The case of John Whitgift is typical.

[1] J. Bass Mullinger, *The University of Cambridge from* 1535 *to the Accession of Charles I*, p. 419.

He was Master of Trinity College, and Regius Professor
of Divinity at Cambridge ; became Bishop of Worcester,
and in 1583 was raised by Elizabeth to the Archbishopric
of Canterbury. Yet Whitgift knew so little Greek that
he was sometimes accused of knowing none at all. A
clergyman called Broughton incurred the Archbishop's
displeasure by certain opinions he had published, and
imputed the prelate's attitude to his ignorance of the
New Testament in the original. " If his Grace had
known any one word in the Greek, as a perfect linguist
should," exclaimed the injured divine, " he would not
so have persecuted my studies."

In the time of Elizabeth and for long afterwards,
University instruction lagged far behind the erudition
attained by private and undirected study. Even after the
humanists of the Renaissance had done their work,
tutors and fellows still continued to neglect the humanities
and to make their scholars grind in the scholastic mill.
University exercises still took the form of public disputations on metaphysical problems, and the more
accomplished undergraduates, like Marlowe's Dr. Faustus,
made the schools ring with *sic probo*. But many young men
fresh from home, looking for poetry and Platonism, were
bitterly disappointed, and chafed under this dry and abs-
truse regime. Milton declares that the Universities as he
knew them were " not yet well recovered from the scholastic
grossness of barbarous ages," that they presented to
their scholars only arid abstractions, " fathomless and
unquiet deeps of controversy " ; and that many acquired
in consequence a hatred and contempt of learning.

Such instruction was as repellent to philosophers as to poets. Hobbes speaks with great contempt of the studies to which he was introduced at Oxford. Logic, with its figures and moods, he learned and cast aside; and the distinctions of matter, form and species he found to be beyond his comprehension. He turned his attention to more congenial studies and read books of geography, voyages and travels.[1]

John Locke had a similar experience. On beginning his residence at Oxford, he found that the chief subject of study was the Aristotelian philosophy, " perplexed with obscure terms and useless questions." The public disputations, the great academic events of the year, in which propositions were advanced and attacked by logical method, seemed to him to be merely wearisome, " invented for wrangling or ostentation, rather than to discover truth." Locke's life as an undergraduate so discouraged him that he began to doubt his own capacity even to be a scholar, and spent much of his time in reading romances.

Whether Shakespeare would have found an interest in University studies, and profited more by them than Milton, Hobbes and Locke, is a question to which some answer may be suggested. In several of his comedies he has set down his reflections on the virtue and the true method of knowledge. Lucentio in *The Taming of the Shrew* has arrived at " fair Padua, nursery of arts," and

[1] T. Hobbes, *Vita*, Latin Words, ed. Molesworth, Vol. I, p. lxxxvi.

is about to institute a course of learning and ingenious studies. He is thus admonished by Tranio :—

" Only, good master, while we do admire
This virtue and this moral discipline,
Let's be no stoics nor no stocks, I pray ;
Or so devote to Aristotle's checks
As Ovid be an outcast quite abjured :
Balk Logic with acquaintance that you have
And practise Rhetoric in your common talk ;
Music and Poesy use to quicken you ;
The Mathematics and the Metaphysics,
Fall to them as you find your stomach serves you ;
No profit grows where is no pleasure ta'en :
In brief, sir, study what you most affect."

Study, as Shakespeare conceives of it, is something free, happy, liberal and enriching ; and profitable only when cheerfully pursued. It is dull and ineffective when concentrated on minute details, or when it gives only a mechanical knowledge of other men's thoughts. Biron, in *Love's Labour's Lost*, exclaims :—

" Study is like the heaven's glorious sun,
That will not be deep-searched with saucy looks ;
Small have continual plodders ever won,
Save base authority from others' books.
Those earthly godfathers of heaven's lights
That give a name to every fixed star,
Have no more profit of their shining nights
Than those that walk and wot not what they are."

If this should seem to suggest that Shakespeare despised study of every kind and manner, we can but reply, in the words of the King of Navarre :—

" How well he's read, to reason against reading."

With such ideals Shakespeare might have been as much disappointed at Oxford as Milton was at Cambridge when the familiar course of application was first proposed to him. Milton found scholastic metaphysics to be *ingenio non subeunda meo* ; and Shakespeare would probably have had the same experience.

III

It has thus far been assumed that Shakespeare was not at a University in his youth ; and it may cause surprise that any doubt of that belief should now be raised. But everything should be tested ; and even the universal and undisputed assumption that Shakespeare never, even for six months, was an undergraduate cannot be passed over in silence. Approaching the matter without prepossession, and asking only for evidence, we can establish one fact at least : William Shakespeare neither matriculated nor graduated at Oxford or at Cambridge ; for his name does not appear in the Registers of Matriculation and Graduation at either University. But this fact is less decisive than it looks at first sight. Dr. Venn of Cambridge, when compiling his *Alumni Cantabrigienses*, lately made the discovery that there were many students duly entered at a College and in residence there who neither matriculated nor graduated. A complete list of Cambridge students was only to be obtained by working through the Admission Registers of all the Colleges.

The monumental instance in point, says Dr. Venn, is that of Oliver Cromwell, who was admitted at Sidney Sussex in 1616, and resided there for a year; but did not matriculate or graduate. The University, as such, has no record of his presence.

The lists of Oxford students which have been compiled by Joseph Foster are based almost entirely on the Matriculation Registers. It does not appear that the records of the Colleges have ever been thoroughly inspected and the names of many Oxford students of the sixteenth century may still be untraced. Sir Walter Raleigh is said by his biographers to have spent some years at Oriel, and his name appears in the College books in 1572; but in the Registers of Matriculation and Graduation it is not to be found.

Until the archives of the Colleges for the appropriate dates have been minutely searched, and no William Shakespeare discovered, it will be impossible to prove from University sources that he was never at Oxford even for a term.

And such other evidence as we possess still leaves the question undecided. A statement by Shakespeare himself that he had no academic experience would be immediately conclusive; but no such statement is known to exist. It is true that Ben Jonson assigns to him " small Latin and less Greek "; but Jonson, from the height of his own laborious and self-acquired erudition, would have spoken in the same terms of many graduates in Arts. The Puritan divine denied Greek to Archbishop Whitgift, who had been Master of Trinity.

" But what," it may be said, " about the passage in
Greene ? " The sentences from Greene so often
quoted by Shakespeare's biographers are discussed in
another part of this book, and here it is enough to say
that Greene attacks Shakespeare as an actor who is now
setting up as a dramatist. Greene, with his confused
and embittered mind, may have believed that anyone
who became an actor degraded himself. But a position
on the stage is not in itself inconsistent with an academic
record. University men become actors at the present
day ; and they did so in Shakespeare's time, as we learn
from *The Return from Parnassus*, where Burbage is made
to say that they have often a good conceit in a part.
Greene does not tell us that Shakespeare had not attended
a University : the word " University " nowhere occurs
in his denunciation. And in any case Greene may have
known nothing of Shakespeare's life before his arrival
in London. We have no ground for believing that the
two authors were personally acquainted.

Still less light is afforded by Greene's friend, Thomas
Nash, who had also adopted the hazardous career of
authorship, and was as jealous as Greene himself of
possible rivals. Like a writer mentioned by Dr. Johnson,
Nash gabbles monstrously, and his meaning is not
always of the clearest. In all his effusions the name of
Shakespeare is nowhere to be found, nor is there any
passage which can be certainly applied to him.

Nash is indiscriminate in his attacks ; and a University
degree is no passport to his goodwill. He falls in wrath
upon *idiot Art Masters*, who mount upon the stage of

M

arrogance, and " think to outshine better pens by the swelling bombast of blank verse." Greene afterwards spoke of Shakespeare in terms which are similar, and almost verbally identical, when he railed against the upstart Shakescene, who " supposes he is as well able to bombast out a blank verse as the best of you." Authors whom Nash and Greene regarded as poachers in their preserves could not escape attack, whether they were University men or not ; and the hostility of these writers is no proof that those whom they lampooned had never been within the gates of a College. Marlowe, to his honour, has left no trace of such animosities. He was not a writer of pamphlets ; and he did not take part with Greene and Nash in their campaigns. It is even probable that he was the *idiot Art Master*, writing bombastic blank verse, whom Nash assailed.

Marlowe and Nash and Greene and Peele figure in familiar works as a group of " University wits," united by ties of friendship, and all regarding the unacademic Shakespeare as an outsider ; but this conception owes less to actual fact than to the fancy of modern literary historians. Nash was accused by Gabriel Harvey of being only a " Grammar School wit," with the merest rudiments of knowledge. He had actually been to Cambridge, but Harvey, himself a Cambridge man, believed that he did not learn much there.

Thus the evidence which is supposed to establish Shakespeare's complete lack of University education gives no certain result, when closely examined ; and little remains but an impression diffused abroad in the century following his own, and associated then with a criticism of his works themselves, their lack of formal dramatic art, according to the rules of Aristotle, and what was thought to be their unregulated originality.

The unities of the drama are certainly ignored by Shakespeare ; but this fact does not of itself establish his non-academic training. The unities are broken as conspicuously in *The Return from Parnassus*, which was composed at Cambridge and performed there before an academic audience. And Marlowe, who was a gradu-ate of Cambridge, treated the classical theory with equal indifference.

Shakespeare's knowledge of Logic might offer a better test ; for no one could then be at a University and be ignorant of it. It is clear that at some time in his life Shakespeare was initiated into the mysteries of Logic ; but he did not hold it in high respect. He uses it only for the purposes of burlesque. It is the Jester in *Twelfth Night* who asks if this simple syllogism will serve ; and Falstaff who ejaculates " I deny your major," in the manner of the scholastic disputant. The clowns make use of deductive arguments and clinch them triumphantly with *ergo*, after blundering into obvious fallacies. But Shakespeare may have acquired his logic at Stratford ; for at Grammar Schools it was sometimes taught.

Another circumstance is more suggestive. In *Hamlet* appears this piece of dialogue :—

HAMLET. My lord, you played once i' the University, you say ?

POLONIUS.   That did I, my lord ; and was accounted a good actor.

HAMLET.   And what did you enact ?

POLONIUS.   I did enact Julius Cæsar : I was killed i' the Capitol : Brutus killed me.

In the colleges of Oxford and Cambridge the performance of plays by undergraduates was then a frequent entertainment. Sometimes a comedy by Plautus or Terence was presented ; sometimes a new piece, either in Latin or English, composed for the occasion. Shakespeare was familiar with this custom, and in the words assigned to Polonius he suggests that the murder of Julius Cæsar had been the theme of a University drama.

In his own tragedy of *Julius Cæsar* he attributes to the dying dictator the words, *Et tu, Brute*, the only piece of Latin that occurs in the play, and evidently used by Shakespeare as a quotation. These were not actually the last words of the authentic Cæsar, which are otherwise reported by Plutarch and Suetonius. It has often been said that they may be a fragment from some modern tragedy in Latin, which had come to Shakespeare's knowledge, and lingered in his memory. He had long been familiar with them, for they are quoted by Edward IV in the Quarto version of 3 *Henry VI* :—

" Et tu, Brute, wilt thou stab Cæsar, too ? "

But no Latin drama dealing with the death of Cæsar had ever been published in England, and Shakespeare cannot at least have read it in a book. He may have

seen it on the stage ; but no play of the sort was performed in his time in London ; although one entitled
Cæsar Interfectus was performed at Christ Church, Oxford
in February, 1582, the author being Richard Gedes.

Scholars have often identified it with the University
play on Cæsar's death at the hand of Brutus which is
mentioned in *Hamlet*, and have likewise found in it
the hypothetical drama from which Shakespeare derived
his *Et tu, Brute*. But *Cæsar Interfectus* was never printed
and sold ; and it is not easy to understand how an
acquaintance with it could be obtained except by witness-
ing the actual performance at Oxford ; or how Shakespeare could have known of its existence, if his own ante-
cedents had been entirely unacademic. Allusions to a
play once exhibited at the University, and afterwards
left to forgetfulness, are very surprising when found in
works written after the lapse of years by one who had
never been there. Had the performance been a cherished
recollection of Shakespeare's youth, the matter would
be more easily explained.

No research has brought to light the manuscript of
Cæsar Interfectus. Only one fragment of it has been
found,—the Epilogue now in the Bodleian Library ;
which does at least give some indication of the style in
which the play was composed. It has a strange affinity
with a portion of *Julius Cæsar* ; for its trenchant, anti-
thetic and *staccato* prose recalls the speech of Brutus in
the Forum over Cæsar's body.

At the time of this performance Shakespeare's age
was eighteen ; if he was ever at a University, for however

brief a time, we may suppose that the University was
Oxford, from its nearness to his native place, and the
fact that other Stratford boys went there ; and that
1581 or 1582 was the date. Marlowe, who was born in
the same year as Shakespeare, matriculated at Cambridge
in 1581.

If it were now to be suggested that William Shakespeare actually did proceed to Oxford and entered in
1581 at an unidentified College ; that he was present at
the performance of *Cæsar Interfectus* at Christ Church
in February, 1582 ; that he did not return to Oxford
in the autumn of the same year, in consequence of his
marriage with Anne Hathaway, which caused him at
once to seek professional employment, and that he then
went back to Stratford Grammar School as a junior
master ;—none of these statements could be proved by
any sufficient evidence at our command. But it must
be added that there is also no means by which they could
be *disproved* ; that the negative is not established ; and
that the question is still an open one.

Too frequently it is assumed that Shakespeare could
have profited little even by his private studies ; and a
school of Shakespearian critics seeks to minimize everything that could show his linguistic attainments or
extensive reading. When it is observed that the plot
of *The Comedy of Errors* is derived from the *Menaechmi*
of Plautus, they argue that a translation of the *Menaechmi*
into English was then accessible ; when his knowledge
of Ovid is in question, they found it in the translation
of the *Metamorphoses* by Golding ; if he reads Mon-

taigne's *Essays*, it could only be in the English version of Florio; if he betrays an acquaintance with Ariosto, he could have got it only through Harrington—even although it can be demonstrated that he knew the *Orlando Furioso* in the original.[1] The craze for translation-hunting has been carried so far that a succession of Shakespearian scholars have traced one of Shakespeare's translations from Ovid,

" At lovers' perjuries, they say, Jove laughs,"

to a version in English by Marlowe which never existed.[2] Had it been pretended that Marlowe borrowed from Shakespeare, suspicion would have been aroused, and some one would have tried to verify the quotation for himself; but that Shakespeare should borrow from Marlowe seemed quite natural.

[1] In *Othello*, where the handkerchief given by him to Desdemona is spoken of, we read :—
" A sibyl that had numbered in the world
The sun to course two hundred compasses,
In her prophetic fury sew'd the work."
And in *Orlando Furioso* (Canto 46, Stanza 80) :—
Una donzella de la terra d'Ilia
Ch'avea il furor profetico congiunto
Con studio di gran tempo, e con vigilia
Lo fece di sua man di tutto punto."
But in Harrington's translation there is no mention of *prophetic fury*.
[2] J. M. Robertson, *Times Literary Supplement*, December, 1924.

It is hard to comprehend why the range of Shakespeare's mental activity should thus be restricted and why there should be such eagerness to explain away his knowledge of any language but his own. By this process we create a Janus-headed Shakespeare—a man of two personalities. He was both very clever and very stupid,—so clever that he could write the dramas, and so stupid that he could not learn a foreign language,—a feat performed every year by many thousands of less gifted minds—or could not understand that it was worth learning.

The plays afford grounds for doubting the assumption ; not only by the Latinized vocabulary, and the use of Latin words in a sense which is uncommon in English and could only have been derived from a direct knowledge of Latin idiom ; and not only by the frequent use of Latin in such plays as *Love's Labour's Lost*, and the occurrence of French and Italian words and phrases ; but still more by Shakespeare's mastery of the English language itself. He has it under the most perfect control ; his diction is copious, rich and flowing ; his range of expression is wide and comprehensive. And this boundless gift of utterance is attained with no apparent effort. A man who possessed such linguistic capacity and displayed it in all his dealings with his native tongue, could master any foreign language in a very brief space of time and with most exceptional ease.

The unwillingness to allow learning of any sort to Shakespeare is in harmony with the romantic conception

of the untutored genius. The very greatest authors, it
is supposed, owe nothing to the writings of others ;
everything comes to them by inspiration ; and the greater
their genius, the smaller is their debt to their predecessors. The more we discount the education they
may have received, the more we exalt their creative
power.

But experience shows that the man who is destined
by Nature to write books begins by reading them. In
his early youth the literary faculty first appears in that
way ; and even when a child his love of books is a
passion. During all his life it remains ; for the power
to interest others is inseparable from a lively interest
and curiosity of his own, which impels him to seek
familiarity with other men's minds. Robert Burns is
the favourite example of the untutored genius ; yet
Burns was an ardent and devoted reader from his earliest
years. With all the limitations imposed by narrow education and physical toil, Burns had an extensive knowledge
of English literature which is revealed in every line of
his correspondence ; Shakespeare, Milton, Addison,
Locke, Swift, Gray, Thomson, Pope, Richardson,
Smollett, Fielding, Shenstone, Goldsmith, Chesterfield,
Sterne, Cowper,—even Donne,—are all familiar names.
He begins a letter thus :—

" Dryden's Virgil has delighted me. I do not know whether
the critics will agree with me, but the Georgics are to me by
far the best of Virgil. It is indeed a species of writing entirely
new to me, and has filled my head with a thousand fancies of
emulation."

Burns also applied himself to French, and in another letter asks a friend to obtain for him a good copy of Molière, also Racine and Corneille. Some of his books are still extant, including a copy of De Lolme's *British Constitution*, which he presented to a public library in Dumfries.

It is not lightly to be assumed that Shakespeare's interest in books was less than that of the Scottish ploughman ; but there is a conventional Shakespeare to whom both were a matter of indifference, and who had no library except a few dog-eared volumes in which he dug for plots. This is another paradox ; as dangerous to clear understanding as most paradoxes are ; and another hint for the anti-Stratfordian controversialist. Baconism will never be wanting so long as Shakespearian scholars cling to their Janus-headed monstrosity.

The belief that Shakespeare lacked education, is supposed to find support in the errors and anachronisms which have been detected in his works. He places harbours in inland towns, and gives a sea-coast to Bohemia, which has none ; he assumes, in the mediaeval fashion, that the manners and customs of the past differed but little, or not at all, from those of his own age ; put clocks in ancient Rome, and cannon in the time of Macbeth ;—all, it is said, as the result of mere complacent ignorance.

This argument is a very fallacious one. If it were applied in a similar fashion to modern authors, of whose history more is known, it would produce results in complete contradiction to the actual facts of their lives.

In a beautiful passage in *The Antiquary*, where Scott is describing the on-coming of a great storm at evening, he depicts the dying splendour of the sun, " resting his huge disc upon the edge of the level ocean " ;—and the scene of *The Antiquary* is on the east coast of Scotland. A sun which sets in the east is something much more startling than a harbour at Verona, or clocks in Ancient Rome ; but the passage has never been cited to prove that Scott was in a state of childlike ignorance, and had failed to master even the simplest elements of geography and astronomy.

His historical novels abound in anachronisms as patent to the reader as any that have been found in *Hamlet* or *Julius Cæsar*. In the introduction to *Ivanhoe* Scott himself remarks,—" I neither can nor do pretend to the observation of complete accuracy, even in matters of outward costume, much less in the more important points of language and manners " ; and he adds,—" It is necessary for exciting interest of any kind that the subject assumed should be, as it were, translated into the manners, as well as the language of the age we live in." There could not be a better description of the method which was also pursued by Shakespeare in his historical plays and Roman tragedies.

The story of *Ivanhoe* has, in fact, no certain period or place. Nominally the time is that of Richard I ; but Scott has introduced the customs of chivalry which belonged to the time of Edward III, and had been made familiar to him by Froissart. In words addressed to a more rigid antiquary, Dr. Dryasdust, he remarks :

" It is extremely probable that I may have confused the manners of two or three centuries, and introduced, during the reign of Richard I, circumstances appropriated to a period either considerably earlier, or a good deal later than that era." He has placed Saxons in Yorkshire where no Saxons ever were, for the north of England was colonized by the Angles ; and has arrayed the knights of the twelfth century in plate armour, instead of chain-mail.

In *Kenilworth* he speaks of gallants who made the Virginia voyage long before Virginia was founded, and who frequented the Globe and the Fortune long before those theatres were built ; and causes his characters to discuss the work of Shakespeare, and to quote *The Tempest* and *Midsummer Night's Dream*,—although the story culminates in the tragic death of Amy Robsart which took place four years before Shakespeare was born.

It cannot be supposed that Scott did not know the actual dates of Amy Robsart's death and of Shakespeare's birth. He was giving a composite picture of the Elizabethan Age, and thought himself justified in making as many of its events contemporary as he pleased. The inference of mere bookless ignorance which is drawn from similar anachronisms in Shakespeare would here be absurd. Scott was a man of vast reading, an erudite antiquary and historian. As for his library, it contained over ten thousand volumes.

In none of Shakespeare's historical plays has he departed so far from historical truth as Browning does in

Strafford. And Browning goes astray even in his own favourite fields. He was an enthusiastic student of Italian art, and actually lived at Florence for twelve years ; yet *Fra Lippo Lippi*, in which he depicts the character of a Florentine painter, is both inaccurate in detail and misleading in its general conception. The artist, in his rambling monologue, is made to speak of a youth who has begun to follow his methods :—

> " We've a youngster here
> Comes to our convent, studies what I do,
> Slouches and stares and lets no atom drop—
> His name is Guidi—he'll not mind the monks—
> They call him Hulking Tom, he lets them talk—
> He picks my practice up—he'll paint apace,
> I hope so—though I never live so long,
> I know what's sure to follow."

Hulking Tom is Masaccio ; but in actual truth it was Masaccio who came first and Lippi himself who came after, and who was the genuine disciple. Browning was so unconscious of this mistake that he refused to admit it, when it was pointed out to him by Dowden.

His Hulking Tom has not become so famous as Shakespeare's coast of Bohemia or his cannon in *Macbeth* ; but Shakespeare would have cheerfully admitted his inadvertence. He knew as well as any man that cannon did not exist in the eleventh century, for he mentions the invention of gunpowder as a novelty in the time of Henry IV. The truth is that any imaginative writer may fall into such errors when his mind is absorbed in the glow of creative effort, and incidental details pass unnoticed,—to be detected afterwards by the microscope of the critic.

VII

FRAGMENTS

The following pages contain fragments from three unfinished chapters, that were to have been inserted between *Family History* and *Things Which Never Were*.

i. GREENE AND SHAKESPEARE

The first printed allusion to Shakespeare is to be found in a strange work, the *Groatsworth of Wit*, by the poet and dramatist, Robert Greene, written in his last days and published after his death in 1592. Greene led a dissolute life, and died in poverty and wretchedness, a broken-down and disappointed man. He had the mortification of seeing a greater poet rising into fame, and could not refrain from a spiteful attack upon him. "The curse and degradation of literature," as Scott remarks, is its jealousy and envy. Greene addresses words of counsel, mingled with insinuations to Marlowe, to two other poets, who may be identified with Nash and Peele. He exhorts them all three to take warning by his own misfortunes, and to have nothing more to do with the stage. Let them write no more dramas, and put no trust in the actors, who will use their labours

for their own profit, and show them in return no gratitude. Greene's words are :—

> " Base-minded men all three of you, if by my miserie ye
> be not warned ; for unto none of you, like me, sought these
> burres to cleave ; those puppits, I meane, that speake from
> our mouths, those anticks garnisht in our colours. Is it not
> strange that I, to whom they all have beene beholding, is it
> not like that you to whome they all have beene beholding, shall,
> were ye in that case that I am now, be both at once of them
> forsaken ? Yes, trust them not ; for there is an upstart
> crow, beautified with our feathers, that, with his *Tyger's heart
> wrapt in a Player's hide,* supposes he is as well able to bumbast
> out a blanke verse as the best of you ; and being an absolute
> *Johannes Factotum,* is in his owne conceit the onely Shake-
> scene in a countrie."

The *Groatsworth of Wit* met in its own day with a
very unflattering reception. Shakespeare was offended ;
Marlowe bitterly resented the allusions to himself ; Nash
described it as a " trivial, lying pamphlet," and utterly
disowned it ; and Chettle, who had taken the responsi-
bility of printing it after Greene's decease, hastened to
withdraw and apologize. The lapse of more than three
hundred years has added obscurity to its original imper-
fections ; but we must endeavour, so far as may be, to
throw light into its dark places ; for there is a familiar
misapprehension of its meaning by which Shakespeare
has suffered, and still suffers, no small injustice.

1. The actors are denounced by Greene as " puppets
that speak from our mouths, antics garnished in our
colours," and Shakespeare, in continuation of the same
idea, as an " upstart crow beautified with our feathers."

His meaning is :—We write plays ; the actors merely perform them. They recite the speeches we compose, and gain distinction which is really due to the author alone ; for in applauding their recitation the audience sees only the actor, and forgets the poet who has furnished his speech. The substance of Greene's complaint is more plainly expressed in a recent novel by Horace Wyndham, where the following remarks are made by a theatrical manager :—

" While you can take any person of ordinary intelligence and teach him to act sufficiently well to make people pay to witness his performance, it's impossible to teach anyone to paint a picture or write a line of poetry unless that person be artistically inclined. Besides, what is acting after all but the delivery of somebody else's ideas ? The real artist is the man who creates something,—that is, in this case, the dramatist. If people who go to the theatre would only realize that, while hundreds of men can play Hamlet—with greater or less skill —only one man has been able to write it, we should have a saner view of the actor's worth."

2. The actors have forsaken Greene in his distress, and have done nothing to relieve him ; and in like manner they would forsake his fellows, were they in the same straits. Here the foundation of the complaint is obviously of a financial nature. The actors have made no contribution to help Greene in his poverty. Could we know the whole story, we should probably learn that Greene had appealed for pecuniary assistance to a company to which he had sold one of his plays ; that they had refused, considering that the piece had already been

N

fully paid for, and perhaps being unaware of Greene's pressing need ; and that his disappointment had inspired him with resentment against the whole acting profession.

3. In addressing Marlowe and the rest Greene states that " to none of you sought those burrs to cleave." He means that the actors of whom he speaks had not tried to cultivate their acquaintance ; and, as Shakespeare is one of the actors, he also is one of the " burrs," and has not tried to " cleave " to Marlowe ; in other words, he has not moved in the same circle, and there has been no fellowship or intimacy between them. This is the natural interpretation of Greene's words, and tends to negate the idea that Shakespeare and Marlowe had ever collaborated in the production of a play.

4. Greene has another and a special grudge against Shakespeare. It is not enough that he belongs to a class of men who appear in plays on the stage, and thus carry away credit and reputation from the authors themselves. Worse remains to be told. The ambitious and conceited actor, not content with acting, has now set up as a poet and dramatist, and fancies himself as well qualified as better men to write high-sounding speeches. Greene even offers a sample of the stuff which the new poet is producing. He writes such stilted and bombastic lines as this :—

" Tiger's heart, wrapt in a player's hide."

The judgment of the reader is invoked and he is asked what he thinks, or can think, of such pretentious rubbish. But Greene has not merely quoted the line : he has deliberately misquoted it, as if such lines were not worth the trouble of accuracy, and in so doing has got in another hit at his rival's profession. In its authentic form the line is—

"O tiger's heart, wrapt in a woman's hide."

It is taken from the speech in 3 *Henry VI*, addressed by the unfortunate Duke of York, before his murder, to Margaret of Anjou, who is exulting over his defeat and ruin.

The line is quoted by Greene as Shakespeare's, as a sample of the bombastic phraseology by which the upstart makes his bid for fame. Shakespeare with his "Tiger's heart wrapt in a woman's hide" thinks himself as well able to compose blank verse as the best poet alive. In the same fashion the critics of more recent times might have written, "Wordsworth with his primrose by the river's brim"; or "Macaulay with his omniscient schoolboy"; or "Matthew Arnold, with his sweetness and light." Such contemptuous quotation is very familiar in politics:—"Mr. Asquith, with his 'Wait and See'"; or "Mr. Lloyd George, with his rare and refreshing fruit"; or, "Lord Haldane, with his spiritual home."

The vital significance of the words *with his*, which are the key to the interpretation of the whole passage, has been so strangely overlooked, and even perverted, that it is necessary to emphasize it. When I say, "Mr. Asquith, with his 'Wait and See'", I mean that it was Mr. Asquith who said "Wait and See." I do not

mean that I said it, or that it was said by one of my
friends, or by anybody but Mr. Asquith. Greene lets
us know that the Duke of York's speech is Shakespeare's,
and that he himself does not admire it. So much the
worse for Greene's critical judgment ; but that is his
meaning. He is not claiming for himself or others the
authorship of 3 *Henry VI* or any share in the authorship. He attributes it to Shakespeare, and is sure that
it is very bad poetry. His criticism does not matter ;
what we are concerned with is his evidence.

This passage from Greene has had such a devastating
effect on Shakespearian study that we cannot but wish
it had never been written or never discovered. Greene's
words are supposed to justify the belief that Shakespeare
began his novitiate as a dramatist by tinkering old pieces,
and pursued that humble avocation before he attempted
to write original work of his own. A critic of real insight
quotes the statement that Shakespeare " being an absolute Johannes Factotum, is in his own conceit the only
Shakescene in a country " ; and adds : " The fair inference is that Shakespeare was known as a sort of Do-all,
a Factotum who could turn his hand to anything, and
that he was successful not only as a writer, but as an
adapter and improver of plays."

This inference, however, is far from convincing.
There is no evidence to show that Shakespeare was
generally known as a Factotum, or that anyone but Greene
himself in this very passage ever applied that name to
him. And there is an unlucky ambiguity about the
word itself. It has now come to mean a man-of-all-

work, a servant who does odd jobs about the place. But it had no such significance as used by Greene, and the last thing he meant to convey was that Shakespeare did odd jobs about the theatre, such as furbishing up old pieces. For Greene a Johannes Factotum is a person of boundless conceit, who thinks himself able to do anything, however much beyond the reach of his real abilities. Shakespeare is one because he is not content to be an actor and aspires to be a dramatist. He is such an absolute Johannes Factotum that he thinks himself the only dramatist worthy of the name in England. " A would-be universal genius " is the definition of " Factotum " given in the *New English Dictionary*, where Greene's words are quoted and explained.

Whilst Greene emphasizes Shakespeare's self-confidence and assumption of superiority, he is actually supposed to mean that Shakespeare occupied himself with the drudgery of revising other men's writings. The original meaning of the words could not be more completely reversed. The man who thought himself " the only Shakescene in a country " would naturally produce original creations, by which he might display his powers and outshine his rivals. But Greene's words have been understood in the sense least suggestive of ambition or originality in Shakespeare, and the interpretation has been repeated from book to book, just as his testimony to Shakespeare's authorship of 3 *Henry VI* has been accepted as a denial of it, and even as a suggestion that Marlowe and Greene himself had something to do with that work, and that Shakespeare when he took it over was no more than a plagiarist. The study of Shakespeare's first historical drama has thus been thrown into chaos.

From the evidence of Greene we know that Shakespeare, and no one but Shakespeare, was the author of the line :—

" O tiger's heart, wrapped in a woman's hide,"

and consequently of the context in which it stands. It is reasonable to infer that it was Shakespeare who wrote the whole speech, and the drama in which we find it, and to cite Greene himself as a contemporary witness to his authorship of 3 *Henry VI*.

ii. 3 HENRY VI

An incorrect and defective edition of 3 *Henry VI* was published in 1595 under the title *The True Tragedy of Richard, Duke of York*, in allusion to its most striking scene, the passage which Greene attacks and despises. Similar mangled versions of other plays have come down to us, among which the *Hamlet* of 1603 is the most conspicuous. They were published without the authority of Shakespeare and his fellow-actors, and owed their existence to the enterprise of pirate publishers, who obtained their mutilated texts by various illicit devices. It is reasonable to consider whether *Richard, Duke of York* may not also be such a piratical publication of a genuine Shakespearian work.

In 1595 Shakespeare's age was thirty-one, and he had

already composed a series of plays both tragedies and comedies. There is nothing in the date itself to stamp *Richard, Duke of York* as a pre-Shakespearian production. Nevertheless, literary historians are almost unanimous in supposing it to be the work of an earlier poet, which fell into Shakespeare's hands, and which he revised and augmented, thereby producing 3 *Henry VI* as it stands in the Folio. Sometimes Marlowe is believed to be the author of *Richard, Duke of York*. Sometimes Greene is said to have had at least a share in it.

In the edition of 1595 the Duke of York's speech appears line for line, and word for word, as it is found in the Folio, with only a few slight variations, which are due to obvious corruptions in the text. In *Henry VI* we read :—

> " But you are more inhuman, more inexorable,
>   O ten times more than tigers of *Hyrcania* " ;

and in *Richard, Duke of York* :—

> " But you are more inhuman, more inexorable,
>   O ten times more than tigers of *Arcadia*."

From a comparison of these passages alone we should be justified in concluding that *Henry VI* itself is the original, that the author wrote *Hyrcania*, and that Arcadia is due to the blunder of a copyist, who was writing when the speech was recited, and was misled by the sound of the word. The poet himself—any poet—must have known that Arcadia did not owe its celebrity to the fierceness of its tigers, but to its pastoral peace and felicity.

Other passages may be compared with a similar result. In *Henry VI*, when Queen Margaret denounces Richard of Gloucester, we read :—

> " But thou art neither like thy sire nor dam,
> But like a foul misshapen stigmatic,
> Marked by the destinies to be avoided,
> As venom toads or lizards dreadful stings."

And in *Richard, Duke of York* the corresponding lines are :—

> " But thou art neither like thy sire nor dam,
> But like a foul misshapen stigmatic,
> Marked by the destinies to be avoided,
> As venom toads, or lizards fainting looks."

There is no cause to fear the fainting looks of any wild creature ; and the editor of the Quarto has converted the phrase into nonsense.

In the following scenes we reach the battle of Towton. A soldier who has slain one of the enemy, and enters bearing his corpse, discovers that the dead man is his own son :—

> " Thou that so stoutly hast resisted me
> Give me thy gold, if thou hast any gold ;
> For I have bought it with a hundred blows.
> But let me see : is this our foeman's face ?
> Ah ; no, no, no ! it is mine only son ! "

The Quarto presents the same lines in this shape :—

> " Lie there thou that foughst with me so stoutly.
> Now let me see what store of gold thou hast.

But stay ; methinks this is no famous face.
Oh no ! it is my son that I have slain in fight."

Famous face is here unintelligible ; and is only a deviation from the *foeman's face* of the Folio itself.

A still more striking comparison can be made. In the last act, when King Edward presents the young Prince of Wales to his brothers, Gloucester says, according to the Folio reading :—

" And that I love the tree from whence thou sprangst,
Witness the loving kiss I give the fruit,"—

which the Quarto presents in this confused fashion :—

" And that I love the fruit from whence thou sprangst,
Witness the loving kiss I give the child."

That this also can only be a corrupt version of the lines in the Folio is manifest.

3 *Henry VI* is the original and genuine work as it left the author's hand,—" the true and perfect copy " ; and *Richard, Duke of York*, although published so long before, is merely a " stolen and surreptitious " version, defective both in metre and sense, one of the Bad Quartos, " maimed and deformed by the frauds and stealths of injurious impostors," which Heming and Condell denounced ;—only that and nothing more.

iii. THE TAMING OF THE SHREW

Besides *The Taming of the Shrew*, first printed in the Folio of 1623, we possess another comedy entitled, with a slight difference, *The Taming of a Shrew*, which was published in Quarto in 1594, without the author's name, but with an intimation that it had been performed by the Earl of Pembroke's Company. Its relationship to Shakespeare's play is perplexing. The two works agree in theme and plot; Christopher Sly appears in both; the Shrew is tamed in both by the same means. In both the husband behaves riotously at the wedding, starves his wife during the honeymoon, and flings away the hat and gown brought by the haberdasher and the tailor. In both the wife makes complete submission, admits that the sun is the moon, and pretends that an old gentleman is a young lady. In some places the dialogue closely corresponds, and even is identical, almost word for word; in others, and for many pages, it is totally different. The names of the characters also are different, with the exception of Kate herself.

Concerning the relationship of these comedies to each other, there are no fewer than *three* possible theories.

1. The Quarto of 1594 was an old work by a different and unknown author. Shakespeare took it over and rewrote it, thus producing *The Taming of the Shrew*, for which he cannot claim the credit of originality. This is the familiar and generally accepted belief; although the date of the Quarto does not of itself suffice to prove a pre-Shakespeare authorship.

2. The Quarto of 1594 was composed by Shakespeare himself, and was his own first draft of the play. This is the theory put forward by Dr. Courthope, and adopted with some reserve by Sir Walter Raleigh.

3. *The Taming of the Shrew* came first, and was an

original work by Shakespeare, with no model or predecessor, except in so far as the story of Bianca and her
lovers was founded on Ariosto's *Suppositi*. Afterwards
another author, desiring to take advantage of Shakespeare's
materials and his popularity, composed the Quarto of
1594. He attended performances of Shakespeare's
comedy, and became familiar with its plot, characters
and situation; wrote his comedy on similar lines; in-
corporated portions of Shakespeare's dialogue which
had lodged in his memory; and drew on his own invention for the rest; producing thus a composite work
partly by Shakespeare, partly by a minor and unauthorized
dramatist imitating him.

If such a dramatist existed Shakespeare was not the
only writer whom he laid under contribution; for on a
close examination of the Quarto of 1594 we find that it
also contains a number of lines copied from Marlowe.
The nobleman of the Induction enters with the words :—

" Now that the gloomie shaddow of the night,
   Longing to view Orion's drisling lookes,
   Leapes from th' antarticke World unto the skie
   And dims the Welkin with her pitchie breath,
   And darkesome night oreshades the christall heavens,"

which are appropriated, word for word, from *Dr. Faustus*;
and elsewhere *Tamburlaine* is similarly pillaged. The
author had evidently stored the beauties of Marlowe in
his mind or in a commonplace book, and worked them
in as occasion afforded.

These borrowings may throw some light on the mystery,

and may be more consistent with one of the three theories than with the other two.

1. On the first theory we must suppose that the pre-Shakespearian author was clever enough to create Christopher Sly, to write his delightful babblings, and to invent the bright comedy of the Shrew and her boisterous husband ; that he had some portion of the Shakespearian spirit ; but that he was so lacking in humour and imagination, so mechanical in his methods as to collect the Marlowe passages and insert them here and there with most incongruous results.

2. On the second theory—that Shakespeare himself was the author of the Quarto of 1594—we must attribute the literal annexation of Marlowe's lines to him. This is so improbable that the second theory may be safely ruled out.

3. The borrowings from Marlowe's tragedies are most consistent with the theory which has been set down here as the third. The author or compiler of the Quarto of 1594 was a man who believed in the motto, *je prends mon bien où je le trouve.* He admired and copied his great contemporaries ; took Christopher Sly and the Shrew and her husband from Shakespeare ; annexed fragments of Marlowe's blank verse ; and embedded his plagiarisms in dull pages of his own composition. Hence the singular inequality of style which appears in the Quarto. Its author is drawing on Shakespeare himself when he writes :—

"Even in these honest meane abilliments,
  Our purses shall be rich, our garments plaine,"

where two lines from *The Taming of the Shrew* are reproduced with insignificant variations. But when he relies upon his own Pegasus he falls into a barbarous jog-trot, of which this is a sample :—

> " Now Senior *Phylotus*, we will go
> Unto *Alfonso's* house, and be sure you say
> As I did tell you, concerning the man
> That dwells in *Cestus*, whose son I said I was."

A comparison of these extracts alone suffices to establish the presence in the play of two different hands.

That the Quarto was written in this fashion by a plagiarist and imitator of Shakespeare seems to be the hypothesis which most easily clears up the affair. If it be accepted, the Quarto will find its natural place among the " stolen and surreptitious copies " put forth by " injurious impostors " of which Heming and Condell speak.

We may believe also that the plagiarist boldly made use of Shakespeare's own title. The difference between *A Shrew* and *The Shrew* is a matter of no importance, and cannot have been intended to suggest a distinction between one play and the other. It is even possible that *The Taming of a Shrew* was the original form used by Shakespeare himself ; we cannot take for granted that any allusion to a play bearing that title must indicate the Quarto version.

iv. THE COMEDY OF ERRORS

The date of *The Comedy of Errors* is indicated by the jesting allusion which Dromio makes to France " armed

and reverted, making war against her heir." The heir
was Henry of Navarre whom the Catholics of the League
sought to exclude by armed force from the succession.
As he inherited the Crown in August, 1589, when his
predecessor Henry III was murdered, the play, it is
assumed, can only have been written subsequent to that
date, probably in 1590 or 1591.

But the struggle for the exclusion of Henry of Navarre
had really begun long before. Shakespeare speaks of
him as *heir* to the throne of France ; and he actually
became the heir on the death of the Duke of Anjou,
who alone stood between him and Henry III, in June,
1584, Henry III himself being childless nor likely to
leave posterity. When the right of succession thus
devolved on Henry of Navarre the Catholic leaders
immediately began their measures of resistance. They
took up arms in 1585, and issued a defiant manifesto ;
Henry of Navarre followed their example and appealed
for assistance to Elizabeth ; the struggle continued
during 1586 ; and on 20 October, 1587, Henry won a
brilliant victory over the Leaguers at Coutras which
sent his fame through Europe.

These events are enough to indicate that we need not
wait until 1589, at the earliest, for the composition of
The Comedy of Errors with its allusion to the civil war
in France.

We may also observe that *heir* to the crown is a designation more appropriate to the period between 1584 and
1589. In the latter year Henry of Navarre exchanged
it for that of sovereign. Although his accession was not

then admitted by the Catholics, he at once assumed the title of Henry IV, and was recognized as King of France by England and the Protestant nations. So far then as the allusion in *The Comedy of Errors* determines the date of the play, it points to a time *before* 1589 rather than after it.

v. SHAKESPEARE'S HANDWRITING

In the Baconian case much has been made of Shakespeare's handwriting, as it appears in the signatures to his will, and to several legal documents, the only examples of it that we possess. The Baconians are accustomed to speak of it as an *illiterate scrawl*, and a further proof that he was no more than a rude mechanic, the badness of his autograph casting discredit on his literary claims.

In Shakespeare's time there were several different styles of writing and the modern hand was only just coming in. The old English script, which Shakespeare himself used, is so unfamiliar to us that it has to be studied letter by letter, by anyone who wishes to read the manuscripts of the period. Ignorance of this circumstance is the simple explanation of the difficulty many persons find in his autographs and attribute to the hideous penmanship of Shakespeare himself. But even when allowance is made for this fact the signatures of Shakespeare are not distinct: they are hastily dashed off, and sometimes abbreviated, done with a few rapid strokes of the pen. But such careless writing is no proof of illiteracy, for great scholars have often written no better: the signature of Erasmus is a stiff exercise in decipherment, and that of Melanchthon is a series of incomprehensible smudges.

Copious and fluent writers, accustomed to make the pen fly over the paper,—authors, journalists and clergymen —are often noted for the badness of their hand. Isaac D'Israeli, in his *Curiosities of Literature*, states that he was intimately acquainted with the handwriting of five contemporary poets, and that one of them, " educated in public schools, where writing is shamefully neglected, composes his sublime or sportive verses in a schoolboy's ragged scrawl." The allusion is evidently to Lord Byron. Anecdotes once circulated concerning the hand-writing of Dean Stanley, which was so crabbed that his own familiar friends could sometimes make nothing of it ; Andrew Lang's manuscripts could sometimes be prepared for the press by no one but his favourite typist ; and it is stated by the biographer of Edward Caird that his hand was " for the most part either illegible or decipherable only by exhausting all the possibilities."

The worst specimen of a man's handwriting is usually his signature—apparently because he writes it so often that he comes at last to dash it off with a fatal swiftness and fluency. Most of us, at one time or another, have received a letter from some unknown correspondent in which the body of the communication itself was written clearly enough, whilst the signature baffled scrutiny. A man of business, accustomed to signing innumerable letters and cheques, may end by reducing his name to a hasty hieroglyphic which is intelligible only to the initiated.

But it may be doubted whether there is actually such a thing as an " illiterate scrawl." A working-man or labourer who is unaccustomed to writing does not scrawl when he has occasion to set down his name. He takes the pen firmly in his hand, braces himself for the effort, works slowly and deliberately, and produces a signature which is cramped and stiff, but usually as clear as print. The process of writing is associated for him with copy-books at school ; and he writes like a copy-book.

Rapid and careless writing is no evidence of defective education. It rather proves that the writer has had much experience of plying the pen. Shakespeare might have written as carelessly as Byron, and as illegibly as Dean Stanley, Andrew Lang, or Edward Caird, and might still be the author of *Hamlet*. Sir Walter Scott remarks in his *Journal*,—" This hand of mine gets to be like a kitten's scratch, and will require much deciphering, or, what may be as well for the writer, cannot be deciphered at all. I am sure I cannot read it myself." To this pass it had been brought by the composition of many thousands of pages.

It may be added that Shakespeare's fellow-actors and first editors, Heming and Condell, made the statement,—" His mind and hand went together ; and what he thought he uttered with that easiness that we have scarce received from him a blot in his papers." This suggests that his manuscripts presented no difficulty to those who were familiar with them.

vi. SHAKESPEARE AND THE LAW

Nothing has yet been said concerning the theory that the writer of Shakespeare's plays shows a very intimate and accurate knowledge of English law, both, it is said, in its principles and technicalities ; a knowledge so perfect that he is never incorrect, and never at fault. Such familiarity with legal terms and procedure indicates that he must have been by profession a lawyer ; the Stratford player is once more discredited, and a new argument found for Bacon.

Much has already been written on this subject, and nothing more is attempted here than to test the theory of Shakespeare's legal acquirements by the touchstone of a single incident, concerning which even the unprofessional reader may form some judgment.

The remarkable case of *Ford v. Falstaff* may be found stated in *The Merry Wives of Windsor* ; the facts of the case being these :—Mr. Ford called upon Sir John Falstaff at the Garter Inn, under the assumed name of Brook. He professed a sudden friendship for Falstaff, professed also to have more money than he knew how to employ, and bestowed a considerable sum upon the knight. The money was given freely as a gift, but with the suggested understanding that Falstaff as a *quid pro quo* should assist him in a discreditable amorous adventure. No witnesses were present at the interview ; and no receipt, bond or other acknowledgment was received by Ford.

At a later date Mr. Ford repented of his generosity, and resolved to recover the sum given to Falstaff by setting in motion the machinery of the law. He affirmed that he had been cozened of the money, and caused Falstaff's horses to be arrested as security for the alleged debt. Meeting Sir John Falstaff, he taunted him with the prospect of enforced repayment, which he declared would be a " biting affliction." Ford had no doubt that he could recover the money. The dramatist also had no doubt.

Now, it must seem that, if the suit had come to trial, counsel for Falstaff might have made out a strong case. He could have argued that the money was offered as a gift, as in fact it was, and that the condition attached or suggested was one which no court could recognize. He could have pointed out that there were no witnesses to the transaction, and no written acknowledgment. Falstaff, in the box, might have supported the plea that the money was accepted as a present ; or, being an unscrupulous witness, might have denied that any money had been received at all, instructing his counsel to take that line of defence.

It appears that Mr. Ford would have failed in his action. But he has perfect confidence of success, and the dramatist expects the audience to share his confidence, and to anticipate no difficulty in making good his claim.

Such legal interpretation may pass muster in the winding-up of a comedy, when the audience is not in a critical mood. But it rather seems that the dramatist has adapted the law to the play, not the play to the law. His attitude towards legal verisimilitude is one of perfect indifference.

vii. The Second Best Bed

Much ingenuity has been expended on the provision in the will by which Shakespeare left to his wife the " second best bed." The purport of this bequest becomes clearer if we consider the conditions under which it was made.

Shakespeare thought of himself as a landed proprietor and the founder of a family. In default of a son, he made his eldest daughter his heiress, and left to her his house and estate. Had some more modern customs then existed he might have stipulated that her husband should adopt his name, and that their children should be called Shakespeare.

In these circumstances his widow would become a person of less importance than the heiress who succeeded him and would have the position merely of a dowager. It was obviously Shakespeare's intention that she should continue to reside in New Place under her daughter's care, and should occupy the room which ranked second in the domestic scale, the best being now transferred to the new proprietors.

More wealthy families have a mansion-house which passes into the immediate possession of the heir at the owner's death, and a smaller residence, the dower-house, to which the widow then retires, vacating her former home. Shakespeare contemplated a similar arrangement, but his means being less ample, he assigned to his widow, not the second best house, but only the second best apartment.

Amongst middle-class people a similar situation may still arise, and for an example of it the reader is referred to Mr. Arnold Bennett's novel *The Old Wives' Tale*. Mrs. Baines, a widow, no longer young, possessed a flourishing draper's shop, and a dwelling-house above it. Her daughter, Constance, married the assistant, Mr. Povey; whereupon Mrs. Baines made over to them both business and dwelling-house and returned to her native village. When she afterwards visited the young people it was considered a great concession and a special act of courtesy, that she was not asked to occupy the second best room, like Mrs. Shakespeare, but was actually installed in the best, which had formerly been her own.

viii. The Lines on the Grave

The authorship of the lines inscribed on Shakespeare's grave is not certainly known. They may be ascribed to the poet himself; or to his son-in-law, Dr. Hall, who was his executor, and arranged for his burial and tomb; or to some unknown poet commissioned by Dr. Hall. But it should be observed that the lines are in the first person :—

"cursed be he that moves *my* bones."

And it seems improbable that Dr. Hall would have thought of such an inscription, as his own idea, without some suggestion or request from the dying man. If Shakespeare made the request, it is probable that he wrote or dictated the lines himself. They flow easily, and seem to be the work of some one who was accustomed to write verse. They have not the stiffness of the amateur.

It is a perpetual marvel to writers on Shakespeare that the epitaph is so inferior in quality : the great poet should of course have prepared one in blank verse as beautiful as the finest passages in *Macbeth*. " Rude lines " is a favourite designation, or mere " doggerel."

The metre of the epitaph is not an uncommon one in Elizabethan poetry. It is that employed in the simple and graceful lines by an anonymous writer which begin :—

> " There is a lady sweet and kind,
> Was never face so pleased my mind ;
> I did but see her passing by,
> And yet I love her till I die."

Marlowe used it in the smooth song which so pleased Isaac Walton :—

> " Come live with me and be my love,
> And we will all the pleasures prove.
> That hills and valleys, dales and fields
> Or woods or steepy mountains yield."

And Ben Jonson has it in lines that will readily occur to the Shakespeare student,—those placed opposite the portrait in the First Folio :—

> " The figure that thou here seest put
> It was for gentle Shakespeare cut,
> Wherein the Graver had a strife
> With Nature to outdo the life,"—

which for the golden cadence of poesy leave something to be desired, and are certainly more open to the censure of the judicious than those on the grave in Stratford Church.

Shakespeare himself occasionally adopts the same metrical scheme. The reader is invited to examine the Epilogue to *The Tempest*, the authenticity of which has never been disputed. It has not throughout the even and regular beat of the epitaph, and many lines are trochaic rather than iambic, but the similarity is undeniable. We may cite the closing allusion to the efficacy of prayer :—

> " Which pierces so that it assaults
> Mercy itself and frees all faults.
> As you from crimes would pardoned be
> Let your indulgence set me free."

These are the last lines of Shakespeare's last comedy. Let us place beside them those which were inscribed a few years afterwards on his grave :—

> " Good friend, for Jesus' sake forbear
> To dig the dust enclosed here.
> Blest be the man that spares these stones,
> And curst be he that moves my bones."

The similarity in structure and metrical movement is so great that we might be reading extracts from different parts of the same poem. It is not asserted that there is actually such identity as to establish a common authorship : but it is evident that the man who wrote the one may also have written the other.

INDEX

217

CPSIA information can be obtained at www.ICGtesting.com
Printed in the USA
BVOW08s2309090914

366196BV00018B/353/P